WRECK
VALLEY Vol II

By Daniel Berg

A RECORD OF SHIPWRECKS
OFF
LONG ISLAND'S SOUTH SHORE AND NEW JERSEY
Foreword by Steve Bielenda

Library of Congress Catalog Card No. 85-73907
ISBN: 0-9616167-3-3

FOR ADDITIONAL COPIES, WRITE TO:
AQUA EXPLORERS, INC.
P.O. Box 116
East Rockaway, N.Y. 11518
Phone/Fax (516) 868-2658

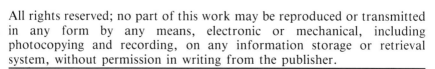

FOREWORD

Being a Northeast wreck diver for the past 29 years has been one of the most rewarding experiences of my life. Meeting Dan and working with him to record on paper the history and excitement of diving New York and New Jersey shipwrecks has certainly fulfilled a dream.

The waters off the Jersey coast and Long Island's south shore, collectively known as the New York Bight or *Wreck Valley*, abound with shipwrecks and each has its own fascinating history and dive conditions. Dan Berg has done extensive research and accumulated an exceptional collection of topside historical photos, as well as underwater and artifact photographs from each site. He's combined these photographs with a well written text to show divers and non divers alike what is sunken in an area known as *Wreck Valley*.

Dan's original *Wreck Valley* book was an instant hit; every diver in the area owns one. It told divers the legend behind each wreck and what to expect on the bottom. *Wreck Valley Vol. II* is even better. Dan has gone all out. He has enhanced the historical information of each story. He covers 32 additional wrecks, has many new historical photographs, more underwater sketches, and has enriched the readers knowledge immeasurably by highlighting the entire text with color photographs. The collection of historical photos alone would take years of archive research to locate and would cost a small fortune if purchased separately. Dan has spoken to many of the east coast's most experienced wreck divers, researchers, and old timers, and combined his own wealth of wreck knowledge with theirs in order to accurately describe each wreck site.

This book must be read by all who have or are planning to dive *Wreck Valley*. Experienced wreck divers as well as the neophyte will find the information rewarding and entertaining. Used as a handy reference manual, checking out facts before plunging down on any wreck, *Wreck Valley Vol. II* will make every dive more exciting and fun.

Wreck Valley Vol. II is the most comprehensive, accurate, illustrated collection of information, photographs, sketches and stories ever written about the wrecks that lie in the New York Bight.

Captain Steve Bielenda, President
Eastern Dive Boat Association.
Owner/Operator R.V. Wahoo

ACKNOWLEDGEMENTS

I would like to thank the following for their time knowledge and information. My wife Denise Berg and Christine Berg for editing and proof reading; Captain Steve Bielenda for his friendship, advice and support; Judy Baird, Ronald Barnes, Ed Betts, Captain Janet Bieser, Ellsworth Boyd, Laura F. Brown, Bill Campbell, Bonnie Cardone, Al Catalfumo, Mike DeCamp, Bill Davis, Captain Billy "Bubbles" deMarigny, Evelyn Dudas, Bill Figely, Eric Garay, Gary Gentile, Hank Garvin, Captain Al Golden, Pete Guglieri, Jean Haviland, Mark Hill, Captain George Hoffman, Al Hofmann, Ann C. House, Rick Jaszyn, Hank Keatts, Captain Howard Klein, Jozef Koffelman, Captain John Lachenmayer, Dan Lieb, Frank Litter, Pete Nawrocky, Captain Frank Persico, Captain George Quirk, Captain Bill Reddan, John Raguso, William Schell, Bill Schmoldt, Rick Schwarz, Herb Segars, Brad Sheard, Jorma J. Sjoblom, Ed Tiedemann, Jeanne Tiedemann, Paul Tzimoulis, Keith Wipprecht, Captain Bill Willis, Chet Zawacki, Charles P. Zimmaro; My diving partners Bill Campbell, Rick Schwarz, Steve Jonassen, Jim Wasson, Charlie "Check" Guttilla, Mel Brenner and Kevin Travell; last, but certainly not least, Winfred Berg, Donald Berg, Dennis Berg and Aaron Hirsh for all of their time, energy and technical advice.

UNDERWATER PHOTOGRAPHY

I would like to acknowledge and sincerely thank all who have donated their beautiful underwater photographs for this book. It is these professionals who made this publication possible. In alphabetical order they are Steve Bielenda, Bill Campbell, Mike DeCamp, Henry Keatts, Joe Koppelman, John Lachenmayer, Tim Nargi, Pete Nawrocky, Herb Segars, and Brad Sheard.

ABOUT THE AUTHOR

Dan Berg is P.A.D.I. (Professional Association of Diving Instructors) Master Scuba Diver Trainer. He is a Specialty Instructor in Wreck Diving, Night Diving, Search and Recovery, Underwater Hunting, Deep Diving, Dry Suit Diving, U/W Metal Detector Hunting, U/W Archeology, and has written and teaches his own nationally approved Distinctive Specialties in Shipwreck Research, and U/W Cinematography. Dan also holds certifications in Rescue and Environmental Marine Ecology. He is the Author of the original WRECK VALLEY book, a record of shipwrecks off Long Island's South Shore, SHORE DIVER, a diver's guide to Long Island's beach sites, co-author of TROPICAL SHIPWRECKS a vacationing diver's guide to the Bahamas and Caribbean, publisher of the Wreck Valley LORAN C COORDINATE LIST, co-producer of the WRECK VALLEY VIDEO SERIES, and SHIPWRECKS OF GRAND CAYMAN VIDEO. His award winning underwater cinematography has been used on a variety of cable TV shows, including LONG ISLAND ALL OUTDOORS, LONG ISLAND FISHING and DIVER'S DOWN. Dan's photographs and articles have been published in SKIN DIVER MAGAZINE, UNDERWATER USA, NAUTICAL BRASS, The FISH-ERMAN MAGAZINE, FISHEYE VIEW MAGAZINE, NAUTILUS plus many more and he is a contributing editor for the magazine SHIPWRECKS.

Dan has made many wreck diving excursions to locations such as Antigua, Barbados, Bermuda, Bonaire, Cancun, Cozumel, Curacao, Eleuthera, Florida, Grand Cayman, Grenada, Jamaica, Kaui, Maui, Nassau, New Jersey, North Carolina, Paradise Island, Pennsylvania, Puerto Rico, Saint Croix, Saint Lucia, Saint Thomas and Tortula. An avid wreck diver, he has always found the Jersey coast and Long Island's South Shore, collectively known as the New York Bight or WRECK VALLEY, to contain some of the most historic and intriguing wreck diving anywhere in the world.

HOW TO USE

This text was designed to be a diver's guide to shipwrecks located off the New Jersey and Long Island coasts. Divers can reference this manual to find information about the history and dive conditions of over 90 shipwrecks. Each listing contains pertinent information such as the wreck's depth, currents, visibility, and types of aquatic life. You will also find many photos, including topside, historical and underwater. Historical information in this guide will help you to have a better understanding of each wreck. Note that many shipwrecks are known by two, three, or even four different names. Some of these names were given to unknown wrecks before they were identified, some are nicknames, and some are the vessel's original name, which had been changed before the ship's sinking.

The easiest way to look up a particular wreck within this reference manual is to look up the name you have for the wreck in the index. I've tried to list all known names for the wrecks.

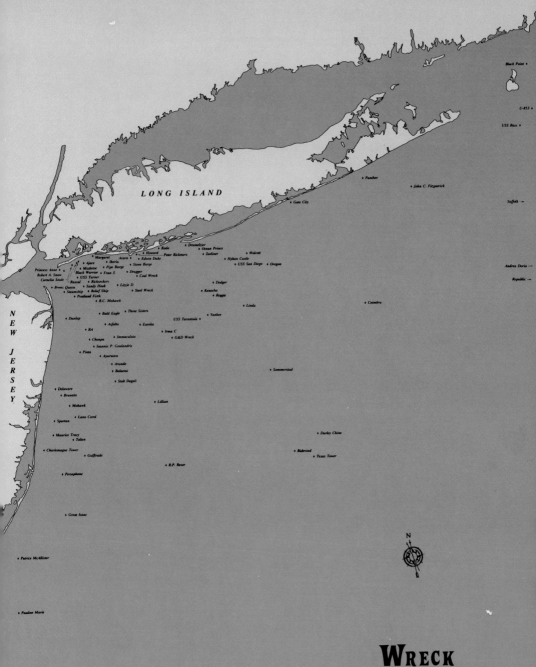

WRECK DIVING

Each year thousands of people all over the world become certified scuba divers. These people have different goals in mind upon reaching their first training certification level. Some want to dive locally all year round, some may only plan on warm weather diving, and others may simply become certified so they can dive on their vacations to the Caribbean. However, there are a large number of divers that have channeled their time and energy into the fascinating world of shipwrecks.

Wreck diving is thrilling for many reasons. Foremost, the thought of finding sunken treasure would be exciting to anyone. Realistically, treasures are rarely found, but wreck dives are like a short visit into history. To explore the nostalgic value of each ship is to realize that the vessel was once built with a specific goal in mind. Perhaps it was designed to be a warship, cargo vessel, freighter or a luxury liner with a crew who lived on board doing the normal things of everyday life. The ship and crew may have suffered a great tragedy. Of course, a sinking that involved lost lives is a disaster incomparable to any other.

There is no dive experience equal to that of slowly descending into the sea with only the noise of your own bubbles around you, and then suddenly seeing a large vessel sitting alone in the sand, seemingly inviting all divers to explore its remains. To observe or photograph an artifact or the large amount of marine life that thrives in and around each wreck is something that a wreck diver can treasure forever.

Contrary to most beliefs, wreck diving is not only for the most experienced diver. Many ships are in water shallow enough for most divers to enjoy, and an exciting experience on a wreck does not have to mean penetration. A lot of wrecks are broken up into huge debris fields scattered over the ocean floor. Others were sunk intentionally with large holes cut through their steel plating, allowing for plenty of ambient light to filter through much of the interior. Wreck penetration should only be done by experienced divers with the proper training and equipment. If good common sense is followed, all divers can enjoy exploring these fascinating time capsules into history.

Wreck Valley

ACARA

The *Acara* was a British steel hulled steamship built by Palmers SB & Iron Company., Ltd., New Castle, England in 1898. She was owned by James Marke Wood, Liverpool. She was 380 feet in length, had a beam of 47.3 feet and displaced 4,193 gross and 2,677 net tons.

The *Acara* broke in two after running aground on March 1, 1902. Photo courtesy Suffolk Marine Museum.

At 2:00 AM, on March 1, 1902, the *Acara*, which is currently referred to as the *Tea Wreck*, was enroute from England to New York with a cargo of 50,000 cases of Chinese tea, 14,800 100 pound tin ingots and an assorted cargo of spices, rubber and gum when she ran aground just east of Jones Inlet during a heavy gale. The crew was able to launch two life boats. The second boat capsized, spilling 17 men into the freezing surf. Fortunately, the life saving crews of both Zachs Inlet and Short Beach Inlet came to the *Acara's* aid, and due to their heroic efforts, all of the crew members were saved. The *Acara* held together for two more days before she finally gave in to the constant pounding of the sea. She broke into two, taking her cargo of imported Chinese tea to the bottom. Within months of her sinking, local salvagers were able to recover 12,000 tin ingots from her cargo.

Today, The *Tea Wreck* lies just East of Jones Inlet, 500 to 600 yards off

Acara or *Tea Wreck* as she is more commonly known rests only 500 yards off shore in 25 feet of water. Photo courtesy Steve Bielenda collection.

the shore in about 25 feet of water. She is mostly broken up, with sand covering much of her ribbing. Parts of her still rise ten to 15 feet from the bottom, providing a good home for blackfish, sea bass, and lobsters. Divers have found all sorts of artifacts on this wreck including brass fittings and spikes, while fishermen can enjoy good fishing close to shore.

Al Bohem with propeller recovered from the *Tea Wreck*. Photo courtesy Steve Bielenda.

AJACE

Also known as the *Italian Wreck*, the *Ajace*, a 566 ton bark, was sunk at 4:00 AM on March 4, 1881. At the time, she was carrying a small cargo of scrap railroad iron and 2,040 empty petroleum barrels. While bound for New York from Belgium, the *Ajace* was caught in one of the worst storms of the year and ran aground off Rockaway beach. Many sources report that Captain F.Morice, seeing that all hope was lost, opened his private supply of brandy and shared it with his crew. Soon after, the crew became badly beaten from the pounding of the waves and drunk from the brandy. Peter Sala, who was the sole survivor of the wreck, told a dramatic story in which he denied that the crew drank from the captains brandy. His story, reported in the NEW YORK TIMES, claimed that half the crew were washed overboard by the heavy sea which poured over her almost simultaneously. Peter and four other sailors, George the cook, Giovanni, Michael, and David managed to hang onto the after part of the vessel. They floated on a piece of wreckage for hours and were beaten, bruised, half drowned, and almost frozen to death. Finally, Michael the ship's carpenter gave up hope. He drew his knife, shouted "come, let us die together", and slit his own throat to shorten his agonizing death. Three of the crew followed the carpenter's lead. Peter Sala was rescued the next day while clinging to the floating ship's cabin.

The *Ajace* now rests in 25 feet of water, 300 yards west of the *Granite Wreck* and inshore from the Warrior bouy. Shifting sands have almost completely covered her, but divers can still find a small pile of railroad rails on this site.

Sketch of the Italian bark *Ajace.* Courtesy Bill Reddan

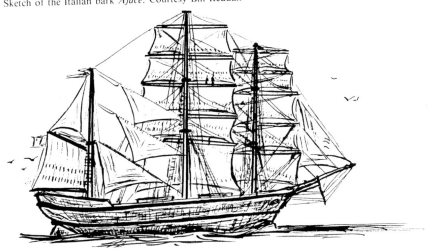

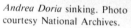

Andrea Doria started to list immediately after being rammed by the Stockholm. Photo courtesy National Archives.

Andrea Doria sinking. Photo courtesy National Archives.

ANDREA DORIA

The *Andrea Doria* was built at the Ansaldo shipyards in Sestri, Genoa, and was launched in 1951. She had accommodations for 1,241 passengers, and 575 crew. She was luxurious to the last detail of her structure and was considered the flagship of the Italian Line. The *Andrea Doria* was named after a sixteenth century prince and admiral, who defended Genoa against her many enemies. The Italian luxury liner was 700 feet long by 90 feet wide. She displaced 29,083 tons, had ten decks, and eleven watertight compartments which extended the entire length of the ship. She was powered by two groups of turbines capable of generating 50,000 hp needed to turn its three blade propellers, each weighing sixteen tons. Besides carrying lifeboats capable of holding 2,000 persons, the *Doria* was completely fire proof and equipped with radar.

At 11:22 PM, July 25, 1956, while navigating through a dense fog, under the command of Captain Piero Calamai, the *Andrea Doria* and Swedish freighter, Stockholm, collided. This disaster has no logical explanation. It could have and should have been avoided, but radar readings aboard both vessels were misinterpreted. The Stockholm, although badly damaged with a smashed bow, remained afloat. The *Doria* suffered a mortal blow; she started to list immediately as water gushed through a huge hole in her

The Stockholm, although being badly damaged with a smashed bow, remained afloat. Courtesy Steamship Historical Society Collection, University of Baltimore Library.

starboard side. The following are radio messages that were transmitted after the collision. At 11:22 (Stockholm) "We have collided with another ship," 11:35 (*Doria*) "We are bending impossible to put lifeboats at sea send immediate assistance," 12:09 (Stockholm)" badly damaged. Full bow crushed. Our No. 1 hold filled with water. We have to stay in our position." Messages continued all night telling minute by minute accounts of this tragedy at sea. Eleven hours after the collision, the *Andrea Doria* was gone. Out of the 1,706 passengers on board, 46 were killed, mostly due to the initial impact of the collision.

Underwater sketch of the *Andrea Doria* as she rests today. © Charles P. Zimmaro 1990.

Steve Bielenda places a commemorative plaque on the *Doria*. Photo Courtesy Bill Campbell.

Bill Campbell and Dave Zubik with windows recovered from the *Andrea Doria*. Photo Bill Campbell collection.

Gary Gilligan and Don Schnell with china recovered from the *Doria*. Photo by Steve Bielenda.

One day after the *Doria's* sinking, Peter Gimbel and Joseph Fox, became the first two divers to visit her. Gimbel located the wreck by finding the yellow bouy left by the coast guard. The two reached her port side in 160 feet of water and began taking pictures. Gimbels black and white photographs were sold to LIFE magazine and appeared in the August 6, and August 13, issues. LIFE immediately hired Gimbel to take additional photographs, this time in color.

In 1973, Peter Gimbel began his work to salvage one of the *Doria's* bank safes. In 1981, not only did he raise a safe, but he solved the mystery of how an unsinkable ship with watertight compartments went to her watery grave. The *Doria* had suffered an 80 foot gash that ripped through her watertight chambers. This gash allowed so much water to enter her hull that the *Doria* listed more than the 20 degrees that this fine ship was designed to handle, so as more water entered, it flowed over the tops of her watertight chambers, thus causing her doom. Gimbel's safe was stored at the New

Andrea Doria

York Aquarium's shark tank, while arrangements were made for it to be opened on national TV. On August 16, 1984, the safe Gimbel raised was opened. The safe contained U.S. silver certificates and Italian notes.

Today, the *Andrea Doria* lies on her starboard side in 240 feet of water. Her hull is now known to a small group of professional divers as the Mt. Everest of diving. Those who dare to explore this wreck must endure nitrogen narcosis, staged decompression hangs, strong currents, sharks, and long surface intervals. Gary Gentile, author of the book *ANDREA DORIA, DIVE TO AN ERA*, has made many such expeditions. On one of his ventures, he and his companions recovered the *Doria's* stern bell. Most divers who visit this wreck are more than happy to recover some of the fine china she once carried.

Gary Gentile with the *Doria's* stern bell.

Janet Bieser, who was the second women to
ever dive the *Doria*, displays two crystal galsses.
Photo by Mark Hill.

Photo by Steve Bielenda.

The *Arundo* was sunk by a torpedo fired from the U-136 on April 28, 1942. Photo courtesy The Mariners Museum, Newport News, Virginia.

ARUNDO

Built in 1930 by the Northumberland Shipbuilding Co. in New Castle, England, the *Arundo* was formerly named the *Petersfield*, then *Cromarty*, and finally renamed *Arundo*. Owned by Hudig & Veder in Rotterdam, she was 412 feet long, 55.3 feet wide, displaced 5,079 tons and was powered by 442 hp quadruple expansion engines.

On April 28, 1942, The *Arundo* was en route from New York to Alexandria, Egypt, via Capetown, South Africa during one of the worst weeks of World War II U-Boat activity. She fell victim to a torpedo which was launched from the German submarine U-136. At the time of the attack, she was transporting two steam locomotives, 123 trucks and jeeps, plus assorted war supplies including bottles of beer. The chief mate spotted the torpedo's track but it was too late. The torpedo hit the *Arundo* on her starboard side. As she listed, one of the locomotives being carried slid off her deck, crushing four crewmen instantly. In total, six members of her crew were lost.

The *Arundo* now rests in an area called the Mud Hole, 25 miles out of East Rockaway Inlet in 130 feet of water. Her structure is somewhat intact, but

The *Arundo's* anchor is a nice photo opportunity. Photo by Brad Sheard.

Divers can still see her cargo of war supplies scattered through out the wreckage. Photo by Brad Sheard.

Bell bearing the *Arundo's* original name *Petersfield*. Photo by Steve Bielenda.

some areas are twisted and decaying, a testament to the corrosive power of the sea. Divers can still see the rusting remains of the two steam locomotives, one of which is located in her aftermost hold buried in debris, while the other is lying on its side in the sand. Jeep tires and an abundance of beer bottles are scattered all over the wreck. Her anchors have remained in the bow of the ship and make for a nice photo opportunity.

ASFALTO

The *Asfalto* is an unidentified wreck thought by some to be a barge which was sunk on March 12, 1932. She lies in 90 to 95 feet of water, just northwest of the *Immaculata* wreck. From my dives on her wreckage, I would estimate that she was a 300 foot long, 40 foot wide, steel hulled sailing vessel. I noticed one mast lying across her remains but didn't find any rigging or brass artifacts. Her bow comes up out of the sand and is still recognizable while the rest of the wreck is very low lying. The most intriguing thing about this wreck, which is also known as the *Cindy*, or *Rudder Wreck*, is the abundance of bottles that divers find on her. The best spot for smaller medicine bottles is on the port side aft of her mast. Captain Bill Reddan told me that one of his divers found a gold snuff box on the wreck, and it is usually a good spot for catching lobsters.

AYURUOCA

The *Ayuruoca*, originally named *Roland*, was built in 1912 by the Akt Ges Wessner Bremen Co. in Germany. She was 468 feet in length had a 58 foot beam, and was powered by coal fired steam.

On June 6, 1945, the 10,500 ton Brazilian freighter, bound for Rio de

The *Ayuruoca* was built in 1912. Photo Courtesy The Mariners Museum, Newport News, Virginia.

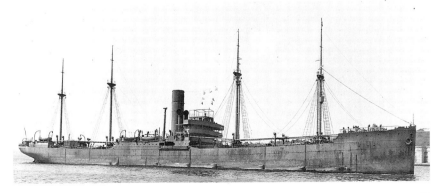

Aerial view of the *Ayuruoca*. Courtesy George Quirk collection.

From left to right Mike DeCamp, George Hoffman, Walt Krumbeck, John Dudas, and Bill Hoodiman with bell and telegraph recovered from the *Ayuruoca*. Photo courtesy George Hoffman.

Janeiro, with lend-lease materials, collided with the Norwegian vessel, General S.S.Fleischer. Both ships had been sailing in a dense fog at the time of the collision. The Fleischer only suffered a gash that was above her water line, but the *Ayuruoca* was not so lucky. Before she sank, one crew member was lost, and 66 others were forced to abandon ship. Eye witnesses said that the vessel sunk within half an hour. All survivors were rescued from their life boats by the Navy Sub Chaser, SC-1057.

It is said that every day since 1945, a few drops of oil float to the surface, hence her new name, *Oil Wreck*. The *Oil Wreck* now lies in an area known as the Mud Hole. She has broken into two pieces that sit between 160 to 170 feet of water, 15 miles off Ambrose Tower. On her decks still remain the cargo of trucks, jeeps, and other wartime vehicles she was carrying. Since this wreck is heavily fished, her upper decks are covered in monofilament lines and nets. Visibility in the area, to say the least, is not known to be great. This wreck is only for experienced professional divers.

BA WRECK

The *BA Wreck* or *B.A. Wreck*, is the remains of an unidentified ship. Her resting place is 14 miles south of Atlantic Beach Inlet, where she sits in 120 feet of water. This wreck has been fished on much more than she has been dived on. In fact, after talking with many local divers, no one could give me a better description of her other than that she's a small low lying wreck.

BALAENA

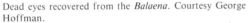
George Hoffman holding the bell from the *Balaena*.

Dead eyes recovered from the *Balaena*. Courtesy George Hoffman.

The *Balaena* is the remains of a wood hulled sailing vessel sitting upright in 160 feet of water. Although her bell, bearing the name *Balaena*, was recovered, no one, to the best of my knowledge, has been able to trace down the history of this vessel or find any reported sinking linked to a ship with this name. Gary Gentile reports in his book SHIPWRECKS OF NEW JERSEY that the *Balaena* could have possibly been a whaling bark built in 1818. Whatever she was, this wreck is well known to experienced deep divers for the abundance of dead eyes that have been recovered from her. According to Pete Guglieri, depth of water at the wrecks deck is 150 feet.

BALD EAGLE

The *Bald Eagle*, a wood ship carrying a cargo of cobble stones, is another of *Wreck Valley's* unidentified shipwrecks. She sits in 80 feet of water, twelve miles out of Debs Inlet. Her true identity or even why she was given her name may never be known. Captain Bill Reddan reports that there is a large ballast pile on the site. He also reports that this wreck has deep holes between her ribs which usually hold a good amount of lobsters. Captain Bill deMarigny tells me that there are actually two wrecks at this site, one sitting on top of the other.

U.S.S. BASS

The submarine, *U.S.S. Bass*, was built at the Portsmouth Navy Yard in New Hampshire. She was commissioned on December 27, 1924, as the *V-2*. The *V-2* was 341.5 feet long, 27.6 feet wide and displaced 2,000 tons. She was armed with a three inch gun, two machine guns, four forward torpedo tubes and two aft tubes. It was not until March 9, 1931, that the *V-2* was renamed *Bass* during a general change of identification. On August 17, 1942, while attached to the Atlantic Fleet, Submarine Division 31, Squadron 3 and on patrol, a fire broke out in the aft battery room. The fire spread quickly to her aft torpedo room and starboard main motor room, all the time releasing toxic fumes in its path. This disaster resulted in death by asphyxiation of 25 enlisted men out of the *Bass's* total crew of 80. The *Bass* was repaired at the Philadelphia Navy Yard. She was then used to conduct secret experiments until December of 1942.

On March 3, 1945, at the submarine base in New London, the *U.S.S. Bass* was decommissioned and stripped. On March 12, 1945, the *Bass* sailed

A torpex filled mine explodes causing the *Bass's* internal hull to rupture. Courtesy Naval Historical Center.

Conning tower. Photo by Brad Sheard.

Diver Gene Howley explores the *Bass*. Photo by Brad Sheard.

Crates marked *USS BASS* photographed by Mike DeCamp when he first penetrated the wreck. Courtesy George Hoffman.

Huge lobster caught on the *Bass* during the 1960's. Photo by Steve Bielenda.

under her own power to the south side of Block Island. The *Bass* anchored in normal diving trim. All nine watertight compartments were sealed. Her final mission was to be the target for a "Top Secret" test of the Mark 24 torpex filled mines. On the morning of the 11th, a PBY (flying boat) from Quonset Point Naval Station took off with two mines. The first mine landed a few hundred feet away from the anchored *Bass*, causing no apparent damage. The second mine landed within 100 feet and caused her internal hull to rupture. The *Bass* quickly slipped nose first into the waves and was gone.

The *Bass* now lies in 155 feet of water, 14.3 miles from Montauk Point and eight miles from Block Island. Divers can reach her main deck at 140 feet. She is broken in two with her bow section approximately 50 feet from her main wreckage. The *Bass* sits upright on a clean sand bottom, and divers report a huge net draped over parts of her remains. This is definitely one of the most interesting wrecks in the area to dive, due to her depth, she is only for the experienced.

BIDEVIND

The *Bidevind* was a 414.3 foot by 55.7 foot Norwegian freighter. She was built in 1938 by the Flensburger Schiffsb Ges ship builders Company in

The *Bidevind* was torpedoed and sunk on April 30, 1942. Courtesy Steamship Historical Society Collection, University of Baltimore Library.

Bart Malone holding bell he and Steve Gatto recovered from the *Bidevind*. Photo by Rick Jaszyn.

Bidevind bell. Photo Dan Berg.

Germany. She was powered by 969 horse power oil engines and weighed 4,956 tons.

On April 30, 1942, the *Bidevind* was en route from India to New York with an assorted cargo when she was torpedoed on her starboard side by the German U-Boat, U-752. The *Bidevind* was then struck a second time. She sunk quickly thereafter.

On September 30, 1943, the *Bidevind* was located 50 miles offshore by the Coast Guard cutter, Gentian. Navy divers explored the wreck and reported that the ship was lying on her side in 190 feet of water and rising to within 142 feet of the surface. Since then, the wreck has collapsed greatly and now lies scattered on the ocean floor.

BLACK POINT

Originally named *Fairmont*, and later *Nebraskan* before being renamed *Black Point*, this steel hulled collier was built in Camden, New Jersey, in 1918. She was 369 feet long, 55 feet wide and displaced 5,353 gross tons. The *Black Point* has earned herself a place in history due only to the time of her sinking.

On May 5, 1945, carrying 7,595 tons of coal, the 27 year old *Black Point* was en route from New York to Boston, and World War II was finally

The *Black Point* was the last ship sunk in American waters by a German U-Boat during World War II. Photo Courtesy National Archives.

Skull and bones inside the *Black Point*. Photo by Bill Campbell.

ending. Adolph Hitler had already committed suicide and Admiral Karl Donitz had issued a personal order to all U-Boats to "cease hostilities". Apparently, Commander Oberleutnant Helmut Froemsdorf, of the *U-853* didn't receive Donitz's orders or simply refused to obey them. At 5:40 PM, he sighted the *Black Point* and fired a torpedo into her stern. The tremendous explosion ripped 40 feet off of the coiler's stern. During all of the commotion, Stewart Whitehouse, a 29 year old oiler aboard the *Black Point*, saw a man hanging upside down by one foot in a fouled rope. Whitehouse managed to cut the man free and then go on to loosen a jammed life raft which prevented more from perishing. At 5:55 AM the *Black Point* rolled to port, capsized and went down taking twelve crew members to a watery grave. The *Black Point* has the title of the last ship sunk in American waters by a German U-Boat during World War II. As for the *U-853*, she was sunk by an American task force shortly after her attack on the *Black Point* and is now resting in 130 feet of water.

The *Black Point* is now resting in two sections. Her stern is intact and sits upright in 85 feet of water. Her bow lies a good distance away upside down in 85 feet of water.

BLACK WARRIOR

The *Black Warrior* was built 1852 in New York at a cost of $135,000 and

Black Warrior

Paddle wheel steamship *Black Warrior*. Photo Courtesy Mariners Museum, Newport News, Virginia.

owned by the New York and New Orleans Steamship Co. The wood ship was 225 feet in length and weighted 1,556 gross tons. Aside from being fully rigged with sails, the 37 foot beam was flanked by two steam driven side wheels.

The *Black Warrior* carried mail, passengers and cargo through her voyages, most of which were between New York, New Orleans and Havana, Cuba.

Sketch of the *Black Warrior*. Courtesy Mariners Museum, Newport News, Virginia.

Her most notable voyage was on February 28, 1854, when she was seized by the newly appointed governor of Cuba. The governor stated that the Alabama cotton on board the ship should have been listed for the Havana customs people. Captain Bullock of the *Black Warrior* tried to explain that since the cotton wasn't being unloaded in Havana, he was within regulations. Despite his arguments, the Captain and his crew were forced to leave the ship while Cuban officials confiscated the cargo. After transferring the *Warrior's* crew to the American steamer, Fulton, which was then loading in Havana, the Cuban officials imposed a $6,000 fine and detained the *Warrior*.

Pro-slavery forces in this country used the *Warrior* incident as a reason to demand war with Spain. Their hope was to add Cuba as another slave territory. Fortunately, Spain surrendered her position and not only repaid the original fine of $6,000 but an additional compensation of $53,000 for the detention of the *Warrior*.

During another journey in 1857, the *Black Warrior* was caught in a furious gale. All of her coal was consumed trying to keep the ship running, while her wheel-house and life boats were knocked away by the sea. According

Sketch of the *Black Warrior* as she is seen underwater. By Al Golden.

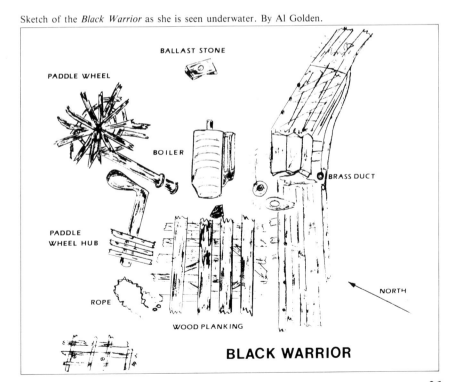

to the NEW YORK TIMES, "Captain Smith manifested the qualities of the cool and skillful." He ordered that all light wood work, furniture and any remaining spars be used as fuel to power her steam engine. His seamanship brought all passengers and crew to safety.

On February 20, 1859, about 9:00 AM, while trying to enter New York harbor in a heavy fog, the captain of the *Black Warrior* ran his ship aground on Rockaway Bar. All passengers, crew and cargo were brought safely to New York by the assisting vessels, Screamer, Achilles and Edwin Blount. At first, she was resting easy and no trouble was anticipated in towing her off. Unfortunately, the *Black Warrior* struck at high tide, and although during the next few days every effort was made to save her, she settled deeper and deeper into the sand. Finally, on February 24, during high tide, she was moved about one hundred feet before grounding again. That same day a gale blew up and the once proud *Black Warrior* was pounded to pieces.

The *Warrior* now rests in 30 to 35 five feet of water. She is all broken up and spread out over a large area. Although most of her brass artifacts have been recovered, lucky divers may still find anything from brass spikes, silverware, and portholes. Take note that the eating utensils found here have the vessel's name engraved on their handles. In the past eight years, we have made many dives on this wreck, and although the site is home to some huge blackfish which would be great for spear fishing, we have always been content to find a spot in the sand and dig for artifacts.

BRONX QUEEN

The *Bronx Queen* is the latest addition to *Wreck Valley*. This 110 foot long, wood hulled fishing boat was cruising off Breezy Point on December 20, 1989, when the Captain heard a loud thump. Within 15 minutes the boat had sunk, leaving 19 people floundering in bitter cold water. The Coast Guard responded and was able to retrieve all passengers and crew from the

Underwater sketch of the *Bronx Queen*. By Daniel Berg.

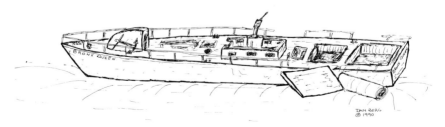

The name *Bronx Queen* can still be read on the wrecks bow. Photo by Jozef Koppelman.

Propeller on the *Bronx Queen*. Photo by Jozef Koppelman.

water within two hours. Unfortunately two of the victims died later in the hospital, one from exposure and the other from a heart attack.

The *Bronx Queen* is a converted Submarine Chaser, possibly the *SC-635*. She was built by Mantis Yacht Building Co, Camden NJ. The *SC-635* was launched on October 12, 1942 and commissioned on October 23. She displaced 116 tons and had a top speed of 18 knots.

On January 6, 1990, less than a month after her sinking, we boarded a charter boat on our way to dive this new wreck. I was the first sport diver to descend. I found a virgin shipwreck, portholes, fishing poles, and brass cage lamps were everywhere. We all had a great dive and will surely always remember the excitement of being the first to explore a new wreck.

The *Bronx Queen* is now resting on a sand bottom only a few miles out of Rockaway Inlet in 35 feet of water. She is sitting upright and leaning on her port side. Her pilot house has been torn away and is now sitting in the sand next to the wreck. At the time of this writing, it is uncertain whether this wreck will be left on the bottom, removed or wire dragged clear so her wreckage is not hazardous to shipping.

BRUNETTE

The *Brunette* was built in 1867 by Pusey & Jones Yards, Wilmington, Delaware.

On February 1, 1870, The *Brunette* was en route from New York to Philadelphia with a general cargo. At 10:00 PM she collided with the Santiago de Cuba.

Captain George Hoffman found this wreck a few years back. When divers started to dig, they recovered crates of brown and white marble door knobs, pocket knives and bottles. All that is left of her is her prop shaft, coal fired steam engine and boilers. The *Door Knob Wreck*, as she is more commonly known, rests 200 feet away from the *Cadet* in 70 feet of water.

CHARLEMAGNE TOWER

The *Charlemagne Tower* was built in 1888 at Quayle & M Co., Cleveland. She was 255 feet long, 40 feet wide, displaced 1825 gross tons and was owned by Southern Steamship Co.

On March 6, 1914, while en route from Norfolk, Virginia, to Boston, she

Today the *Charlemagne Tower* sits in 55 feet of water. Courtesy Steamship Historical Society Collection, University of Baltimore Library.

started to take on water. Captain Simmons ran her toward shore, then gave the order to abandon ship. All of the 17 men aboard departed in two lifeboats. One boat with four on board made it to shore despite a heavy surf. Captain Simmons and twelve crewmen were less lucky. They survived for twelve hours in a rough sea with snow and freezing temperatures acting against them before they were finally rescued by the vessel Bayport.

Today the *Charlemagne Tower* sits in 55 feet of water. Her wood hull is collapsed and low lying but is none the less interesting to explore.

CHARLES E. DUNLAP

This wreck is also known as the *Coconut Wreck*. She was a four masted schooner, launched as the *Myrtle Sawyer*, on November 24, 1904, in Millbridge, Maine, by the Warren Sawyer Co. She weighed 1,498 gross tons, was 224.8 feet long and 42 feet wide. A year later she was abandoned in an easterly gale and towed to Savannah. Many years later she was renamed *Forest City*. In 1916, the ship caught fire while in San Jaun where her hulk was sold, rebuilt and renamed, *Charles E. Dunlap*.

On July 22, 1919, on her first voyage as the *Charles E. Dunlap*, while trying to enter New York harbor ending her voyage from San Juan, Captain Richard Crapsey lost his bearings due to a heavy fog and ran aground on

Charles Dunlap

Charles E. Dunlap aground on Rockaway Shoal. Photo courtesy Art Pearsall.

Rockaway Shoal. Although there were calm seas, the *Dunlap* was unable to be saved. She remained on Rockaway Shoal until she broke up.

The *Dunlap* was carrying a cargo of coconuts during her last voyage, hence the name *Coconut Wreck*.

CHOAPA

Originally named the *Helga*, this ship was built at the Helsingors Jernsk & Msk building yard in 1937. The *Choapa* was 292 feet long, 41 feet wide and displaced 1,700 gross tons.

During World War II, German U-Boats were reeking havoc all along the U.S. eastern seaboard. In order to minimize the chances of attack, merchant vessels were forced to travel in convoys and run at night without navigational lights.

On September 21, 1944, while the *Choapa* was part of an inbound convoy, she was anchored and waiting for permission to enter New York Harbor when the British tanker, Voco, part of an outbound convoy, collided with her. Fortunately, all of the *Choapa's* crew were transferred to the Voco, which was not seriously damaged in the collision, before the *Choapa* slipped beneath the waves.

Today, the *Choapa* lies twelve miles off Asbury Park in an area called the

The *Choapa* was sunk after a collision on September 21, 1944. Photo courtesy Frank Persico.

Mud Hole. This wreck is only for the experienced deep diver to explore. Although she is sitting upright in 195 feet of water, she can be reached at about 160 feet. Visibility is known to be poor, sometimes no more than one or two feet and the wreck is covered in nets and high test monofilament. The divers that I've spoken to that visit this wreck refer to her as deep, dark and dangerous.

Telegraph recovered from the *Choapa*.
Photo courtesy George Hoffman.

Bell from the *Choapa*.
Photo by Daniel Berg.

COAL WRECK

The *Coal Wreck* appears to be the remains of a barge approximately 70 feet long by 30 feet wide. According to Captain John Lachenmayer, she sits in 70 feet of water and has become a decent lobster wreck.

A short distance away, approximately 300 feet, is the remains of another wreck. On this site, divers will find a large fluted anchor, a pile of anchor chain and a deck winch. The area has a slightly silty bottom. Although a bell was recovered from this site, it had no markings that would help to identify her.

Steve Bielenda with bell recovered from the *Coal Wreck*. Photo by Daniel Berg.

COIMBRA

The *Coimbra* was built by the Howaldj Swerke Co., of Kiel, Germany, in 1937. She was a tanker owned by the Socony Vacuum Oil Co., Ltd., of Great Britain. She was 423 feet long, had a 60 foot beam, displaced 6,768 gross and 3,976 net tons.

At 3:00 AM, January 15, 1942, on a foggy morning, a torpedo fired from the U-123 hit her amidships, exploding her cargo of 81,000 barrels of fuel oil into flames. A second series of explosions ripped the *Coimbra* into three

29

The tanker *Coimbra*, sunk by a torpedo on the morning of January 15, 1942. Photo courtesy Peabody Museum, Salem, Mass.

Artifacts from the *Coimbra* are proudly displayed after a 1987 trip to the wreck. Photo courtesy Mark Hill.

Helm from the *Coimbra* hangs upside down, waiting to be hoisted aboard the dive boat. Photo by Gary Gentile.

Keith Wipprecht and telegraph he recovered from the *Coimbra* in 1987.

Dan Berg with a *Coimbra* swing plate recovered in 1987. Photo by Steve Bielenda.

sections before sending her to the bottom. Captain J.P.Barnard, and 34 crew members were killed during the initial explosions and resulting fires. Only six people survived. The NEW YORK TIMES reported with headlines "New U-Boat Victim Confirmed By Navy". The *Coimbra* was World War II's second U-Boat sinking off the eastern seaboard.

Today, the *Coimbra* still lies in the three sections she was blown into. Her bow is facing east, mid section is leaning to port and her stern rests on its side. The wreck is located 64 miles southeast of Jones Inlet and 78 miles from Manasquan Inlet in 180 to 190 feet of water. The *Coimbra* has also created some controversy. Even though the U.S. government has inspected the wreck and issued a report that the oil left on *Coimbra* presents no pollution threat to U.S. shores, others believe differently. In fact, one article about the site reports that there could be as much as 28,500 barrels of lube oil remaining on the wreck. When I first journeyed to this wreck aboard the R.V. Wahoo, we couldn't help to notice the oil slick still hovering over the wreck. The oil is slowly escaping, but over a period of years as her metal decays, this sunken tanker and others like her could cause our beaches to be covered in oil. Even with oil leaking from her hull, I was amazed at the water clarity on this site. We reached her hull at 165 feet and peered over her side to see a row of portholes in the sand in 187 feet. The sand is clean and white, and the marine life over and around the wreck abounds.

CORNELIA SOULE

The *Cornelia Soule* was a 306 ton three-masted schooner. She was bound from Maine to Philadelphia, heavily loaded with a cargo of cut granite jetty stones at the time of her demise.

On April 26, 1902, during a heavy sea and gale force wind, the vessel ran aground on Rockaway Shoals. Because of the heavy sea, lifesavers could not reach the schooner until the next morning. At that time, Captain Bennett and his entire crew of five men were rescued and treated for exposure ailments.

Because of the cargo she was carrying, this wreck is better known as the *Granite Wreck*. She lies inshore and west of the Warrior Bouy in 25 feet of water. Most of her wood hull has become deteriorated or buried, but some ribs and planking can be seen on the west side of the wreck. The stern can be distinguished by some remaining steering machinery, but most of the wreck left to be explored is her cargo of granite slabs. This little wreck has become a good spot for spear fishing, especially blackfish. She has also been a fairly productive, shallow water site for lobsters.

The *Cornelia Soule* was bound from Maine to Philadelphia when she ran aground on Rockaway Shoal. Courtesy Suffolk Marine Museum, Sayville, New York.

Underwater sketch of the *Granite Wreck*. By Daniel Berg.

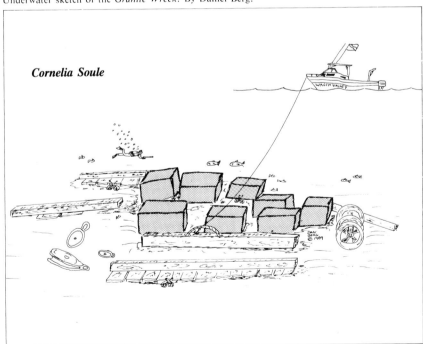

Clyde Line steamer *Delaware*. Courtesy Mariners Museum, Newport News, Virginia.

DELAWARE

The *Delaware* was a 250 foot long by 37 foot wide Clyde Line steamer that displaced 1,646 gross tons. She was built in 1880, by Birely, Hill & Streaker, in Philadelphia.

On July 9, 1898, the *Delaware*, which had recently been refitted to accommodate passengers, was steaming five miles offshore. At 10:00 PM, the captain received a report that there was a fire in her hold. The crew tried to contain the blaze, but it was soon apparent that the fire was out of control. Captain A.D. Ingram gave the order to abandon ship. His crew of 38 and all of the 35 passengers calmly boarded her life boats. By this time, the entire ship was on fire and nearby vessels came to her assistance. Captain Ingram was the last to leave the sinking ship. Aside from a few burns, there were no serious injuries.

The *Delaware's* still floating hulk was taken in tow by one of Merrit Chapman's tugs, but she slipped beneath the waves before making it to shore.

Today, this wreck is very popular with New Jersey divers. She is located in 65 to 70 feet of water about two miles off Bay Head, New Jersey. Her broken down charred remains hold many interesting artifacts. The

Bill Davis with the bell he recovered from the *Delaware* in 1989.

Delaware was also rumored to be carrying $250,000 in gold bouillon. I first dove this wreck aboard George Hoffman's boat. By digging, Bill Campbell and I were able to find a few old bottles. What made the bottles from this site interesting was that they were fused together by the intense heat of the fire that sunk the *Delaware.*

In the fall of 1989, Bill Davis found and recovered the *Delaware's* brass bell.

Sketch of the *Delaware* as she rests today. By Al Hofmann.

S.S. DELAWARE

Daniel Berg with eight pound lobster caught on the *Dodger*. Photo by Bill Campbell

DODGER

The *Dodger* is an unidentified wreck. she received her name from a fishing boat captain who found her on the day the Dodgers won the pennant.

The *Dodger* sits in 100 feet of water. She is a very big wooden wreck, which is mostly broken up, very low lying and provides excellent lobstering. The first time I dove this wreck, I caught a 14 pound lobster. The next visit produced an eight pounder, while on the third I came home with another eight pounder. The ribs of this wreck provide the perfect home for lobsters. Most charters don't run trips to the *Dodger* on a regular basis because her remains are too small for large groups of divers to explore, thus giving the lobsters a chance to grow large.

DRAGGER

This unidentified commercial fishing dragger is sitting upright and intact with a slight starboard tilt in 60 feet of water. She is located only a few miles south of Jones Inlet. In her stern is an "A" frame which rises about 20 feet off her deck. Her bow rests on a clay bottom, and her port side is sunk to her deck in sand. With good visibility, this wreck, which is also called the *Jackie*, could be nice for wide angle photographs.

Kevin Travell with lobster caught on the
Dragger. Photo by Daniel Berg.

Dan Berg holding a brass spot light
recovered from the *Dragger*. Photo
by Mel Brenner.

Sketch of the *Dragger* drawn by Dan Berg and Mel Brenner

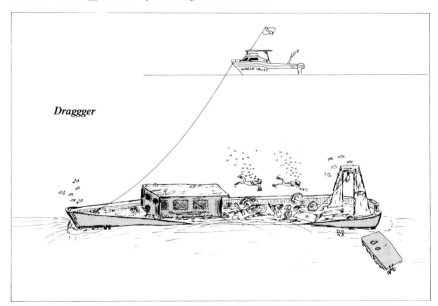

The *Drumelzier* aground on Fire Island Bar. Courtesy Suffolk Marine Museum, Sayville, New York.

DRUMELZIER

The *Drumelzier*, a British freight steamship, was built by Chadwick and Sons back in 1895. Owned and operated by Astral Shipping Company of Liverpool, the single funneled vessel was 340 feet long, had a 44.7 foot beam, was powered by 303 nhp triple expansion engines, and displaced 3,625 tons.

On December 26, 1904, while steaming from New York to Sawansea, the *Drumelzier* ran aground on Fire Island Bar. Attempts were made to tow her off, but they all failed. On December 28, while all but 15 crew members were brought ashore by the tug, Catherine Moran, a violent gale began. Later that day, with the wind still increasing, the *Drumelzier* began to break up. The 15 remaining crew managed to get a life boat launched and were pulled to shore by the lifesavers. By daybreak, the *Drumelzier* and her cargo of copper, steel, oil, pig lead, and one fancy automobile were sitting on the sandy bottom.

Today, the *Drumelzier* has worked its way inshore and is partly visible from the beach at Robert Moses State Park. She now sits in 15 to 20 feet of water with her bow facing east. This wreck is also known as *Quadrant Wreck* and *Fire Island Wreck*.

DUNLAP

This wreck is said to be the remains of a liberty ship. She sits in 50 to 60 feet of water off the Jersey highlands. In her stern divers can see one blade of her steel propeller sticking out of the sand. Her stern is also covered in fish nets. Boilers are recognizable amidships. This wreck is large and well flattened out. Her steel hull plates are spread out into an unrecognizable pattern.

DURLEY CHINE

The *Durley Chine* was built in Sunderland, England, by the Osbourne, Grahm and Co. shipbuilders in 1913. Her 279 foot length and 40.1 foot beam were powered by 209 nhp triple expansion engines. She displaced 1,918 gross and 1,157 net tons and was registered in Cardiff, Wales.

On April 22, 1917, only four years after she was built, the *Durley Chine* was in a collision with the British steamer, Harlem, and sank in an area known as *Wreck Valley*. At the time of her demise, she was en route from Halifax, N.S., to Norfolk, Virginia, under the command of Captain F.J. Anstey. The *Durley Chine's* entire crew of 28 men were rescued by the Harlem.

For some years now, the unidentified wreck, known as the *G&D*, has been thought to be the *Durley Chine*. This assumption was proven wrong on June 28, 1987. A group of divers from the Atlantic Wreck Divers Club, ran an expedition to the wreck which was then known as *Bacardi*. According to Brad Sheard, the *Bacardi* received its name by the charter captain who originally found the site. In order to return to the spot again he marked the wreck with a weighted line and a marker made from a corked bottle of Bacardi Rum. The wreck has since then been known to local divers and fisherman as the *Bacardi*.

Rick Jaszyn, who is one of the east coast's most experienced wreck divers, and a member of the Atlantic Wreck Divers Club, found and recovered the ship's bell. Inscribed on it were the words, "S.S. *Durley Chine-1913-Cardiff.*" This artifact, a prized find for any diver, positively identified the formerly known *Bacardi* wreck as the *Durley Chine*, a Canadian cargo vessel.

Rick Jaszyn holds bell he
recovered from the
Durley Chine. Photo by
Mark Hill.

Today, the wreck lies upright in 185 feet of water, bow and stern intact. Her boilers are amidships and her stern leans slightly to her port side. Visibility on this and the nearby *Texas Tower* can be excellent.

EDWIN DUKE

The *Edwin Duke* is a tug boat wreck. This wreck lies one mile northeast of the *Stone Barge* in about 52 feet of water. Her super structure is completely gutted, but her remains attract good amounts of blackfish during the summer months.

Rare photograph of the tug boat *Edwin Duke*. Photo courtesy Frank Persico collection.

Although I have been able to find no documentation as to the date or cause of her sinking, Captain Frank Persico, tells me the following story that was. told to him by the late Al Bohem, a noted wreck diver and local historian.

Around the year 1930, the *Edwin Duke* was towing a barge with a load of stones to be used on one of the Jones Beach jetties. The tug and barge were caught in a storm. Apparently, the barge began to take on water and was soon dragging the *Edwin Duke* under. In a last ditch effort the crew of the *Duke* cut the barge free. The barge has now become known as the *Stone*

41

Barge and is a popular lobster dive. Unfortunately, it was too late for the little tug. Instead of staying afloat, she inevitably sunk.

The bow of the *Edwin Duke* is now lying on its port side on a sand and mud bottom. A trawler's net covers some of the wreck's starboard bow. Amidships, there is no recognizable super structure. In the vessel's stern, her rudder stands up in the sand. This wreck has been picked pretty clean, but she still produces an occasional porthole, lobsters, some small brass artifacts and lots of anchors. The anchors, from private fishing boats, get caught in the net that is draped over part of the wreck and must then be cut out.

In July of 1989, Rick Schwarz and I dove the *Duke*. I was swimming along her port side when I saw a round flat rim sticking out of the mud. I pulled on it and felt around it. It was hinged to a solid swing plate. My imagination ran a little wild. I thought I had found an intact port hole. Visibility by now was only inches due to the kicked up sediment. I pulled as hard as I could, and the port hole slid out of the mud. Quickly dragging it away from the poor visibility, I found that my prized artifact was not a port hole as I had hoped, but rather a worthless toilet seat and cover. You can't win them all.

Dan Berg with brass pulley, clock and anchors recovered from the *Edwin Duke* in 1989. Photo by Rick Schwarz.

EUREKA

The *Eureka*, a 128 foot tug boat, was built in Philadelphia, Pennsylvania, in 1898. The original owners were the Staples Coal Co., Fall River. Massachusetts. However, the last owners listed in Lloyd's Register are Martin Marine Transportation Co., Inc., Philadelphia. She had a 26 foot beam and weighed 353 gross tons.

The wreck we know as *Eureka* sits in 110 feet of water, 16 miles south of Jones Inlet. A few years ago, either in 1981 or 1982, a couple of local divers recovered a nice relic from the wreck when they were able to cut off and raise her five foot diameter bronze propeller. According to Captain George Quirk, this wreck is not really the tug boat *Eureka*, but an unidentified clam dredge. His reasoning is the lack of towing bits on the wreck, plus the remains of fishing gear. I would have to support George's conclusion due to the fact that there is no listing of a vessel sinking with the name *Eureka* in the area, and upon further investigation and with the assistance of marine historian, Bill Schell, I have located a record in Lloyd's Register that the *Eureka* was dismantled in 1950.

Whatever she is, the wreck known as *Eureka*, which is also called *Broadcast* or *Broadcoast*, is a magnificent wreck dive. She lies in a straight line, her boilers sticking up eight to ten feet off the bottom. Her engine is upright and her prop shaft is easily recognizable. There is also a steam winch sitting in the sand off her starboard side. This wreck has become known for the abundance of bottles recovered around her.

Tug boat *Eureka*. Courtesy Suffolk Marine Museum, Sayville, New York.

FISH HAVENS (ARTIFICIAL)

Along Long Island's South shore and the Jersey coast there are artificial Fish Havens. Long Island has six artificial reefs. Rockaway Beach, Atlantic Beach, Fire Island, Great South Bay, Moriches, and Shinnecock. New Jersey has eight man made reefs. Sandy Hook, Shark River, Sea Girt, Garden State Reef North, Garden State Reef South, Atlantic City, Ocean City, and Cape May. The following is an account of materials used and information on these reefs.

Barge on its way to be sunk as an artificial reef. Photo Steve Bielenda.

Long Island Reefs

1) Rockaway Beach—30 to 45 feet deep
   Reef Materials (a) 2,000 tire pyramids, each consisting of 3 tires
   (b) 420 tons of concrete culvert pipe, 12″ to 72″ in diameter
   (c) Eight barges of concrete rubble
   (d) 60 steel buoys
   (e) 25 barge loads of tunnel rock
2) Atlantic Beach—55 to 70 feet deep
   Reef Materials (a) Seven barge loads of car bodies, total 404 cars
   (b) 200 tons of concrete culvert
   (c) 35 tire pyramids, each consisting of twelve tires

Crane Barge sinking at the Atlantic Beach Fish Haven.

         (d) One 40' by 170' barge
         (e) One 20' by 45' barge
         (f) 10 Good Humor trucks
         (g) Five 34' by 90' wood barges
         (h) Three 34' by 100' steel barges

On October 16, 1986 a steel hulled crane barge, 100 feet long by 33 feet wide, displacing 250 tons was sunk near the bouy four fish haven. She now rests in 60 feet of water and rises ten feet off the bottom.

3)   Fire Island—65 to seventy feet of water
      Reef Materials (a) 9 barge loads rock and rubble
                (b) 1500 car tires
                (c) Two 30' by 90' wood barges
                (d) One 34' by 110' wood barge
                (e) One 40' by 170' steel barge
                (f) Four 34' by 90' wood barge
                (g) One 50' by 14' steel dredge

4)   Great South Bay—16 to 26 feet of water
      Reef Materials (a) two wood barges
                (b) 20,000 concrete blocks
                (c) 1,150 three tire units
                (d) 950 tons concrete culvert pipe

5)   Moriches—70 to 75 feet deep
      Reef Materials (a) 28' wood boat
                (b) 32' wood boat

> (c) 600 auto tires units 3–6 tires per group

6) Shinnecock—80 feet deep
> Reef Materials (a) 6,000 auto tires units, 3–8 tires per unit
> (b) One 33′ by 110′ wood barge
> (c) One 33′ by 90′ wood barge
> (d) Steel bridge structure

In December, 1987, three decommissioned vessels, donated by local businessmen, were added to the Shinnecock fish haven when they were sunk 2.7 miles southeast of Shinnecock Inlet. The vessels were a 73 foot, steel hulled tugboat, a 60 foot steel dredge and a 46 foot, steel hulled cruiser.

Dan Berg holding lobster caught on Rockaway Fish Haven. Photo by Steve Jonassen.

New Jersey Reefs

1) Sandy Hook—40 to 60 feet deep
> Reef Materials (a) 11,230 cu. yards of concrete rubble
2) Shark River—120–135 feet of water.
> Reef Materials (a) One 250 foot barge, *"Coney Island"*
> (b) One 160 foot tanker, *"Alan Martin"*
> (c) One 160 foot tanker, *"Sam Berman"*
3) Sea Girt—60–70 feet deep
> Reef Materials (a) One 100 foot Dry Dock barge
> (b) One 200 foot Railroad barge
> (c) One 70 foot clam boat, *"Carlson II"*
> (d) One 205 foot ferry, *"Cranford"*

(e) One 85 foot tug, "*Spartan*"

(f) One 95 foot tug, "*Rockland County*"

(g) One 75 foot trawler, "*Kiley B*"

(h) One 130 foot barge

(i) One 270 foot car float barge

(j) 13,400 cu. yards of bridge rubble

4) Garden State North—65–78 feet of water

Reef Materials (a) One 52 foot charter boat, "*Good Times*"

(b) One 80 foot barge, "*Shirley Ann*"

(c) One 31 foot cruiser, "*Queen Mary*"

(d) One 247 foot tanker, "*A.H. Dumont*"

(e) One 166 foot freighter, "*Fatuk*"

(f) One 110 foot barge

(g) One 250 foot barge

(h) 626 tire units

5) Garden State South—57–63 feet deep.

Reef Materials (a) One 50 foot crew boat, "*Rhino*"

(b) 1,987 tire units

6) Atlantic City—75–95 feet of water

Reef Materials (a) One 165 foot freighter, "*Pauline Marie*"

(b) One 125 foot schooner, "*American*"

(c) One 265 foot tanker, "*Morania Abaco*"

(d) One 93 foot clam dredge, "*First Lady*"

(e) One 247 foot tanker, "*Francis S. Bushey*"

(f) One 122 foot calm dredge, "*Nilis S*"

(g) 500 tire units

7) Ocean City—55–65 feet deep

Reef Materials (a) 3,045 tire units

(b) Three 41 to 46 foot boat molds.

8) Cape May—50–75 feet deep.

Reef Materials (a) One 106 foot clam dredge, "*Laita*"

(b) One 56 foot landing craft, "*Peggy Diana*"

(c) 26,000 cu. yards bridge rubble

(d) 3,017 tire units

FRAN S

The *Fran S* was an 84 foot tug boat built in 1899. She sank in Jones Inlet during a dredging operation in the early 1970's. Sunk in 18 to 20 feet of water, the tug was a hazard to navigation, but after four unsuccessful salvage attempts, she remained in the same spot. Two years later, she was finally raised off the bottom, towed out to sea and resunk on the southwest corner of the Atlantic Beach Fish Haven.

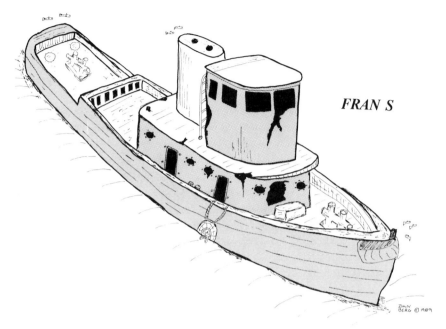

FRAN S

Sketch of the *Fran S* on the bottom. By Daniel Berg.

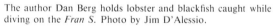

The author Dan Berg holds lobster and blackfish caught while diving on the *Fran S*. Photo by Jim D'Alessio.

Bow of the tug boat *Fran S*.
Photo by Jozef Koppelman.

This picturesque little three dimensional wreck has always brought back fond memories to me. When I first learned how to dive, this was the only wreck I could find without any sophisticated electronics like a loran or depth recorder. My buddies and I would just take a compass heading off bouy four and drag a grappling hook around for a while. In some cases, we would swim down bouy four's mooring chain to the cement block holding her in place, then navigate to the wreck, leaving a tether line to allow us to return to the chain. I wouldn't recommend either method to anyone. We spent so much time looking for the wreck that I've come to the conclusion it would have been much more time efficient to travel on one of the charter boats.

The *Fran S now* sits upright in 70 to 80 feet of water, six miles out of Debs Inlet. Her hull serves as an artificial reef, providing refuge for a wide array of aquatic life as well as an interesting dive location. The area is excellent for big blackfish and sea bass. It's almost commonplace for divers to see eight to twelve pound blackfish swimming in and out of her upper structure.

GATE CITY

The *Gate City* was a Savannah Line iron freight steamer built in 1878, by J. Roach & Son, Chester, Pennsylvania. She was 254 feet long, 38.7 feet wide, displaced 1,997 gross tons, and was powered by a single screw

Wreck of the *Gate City*. Note the man being transported to shore by means of a breaches bouy. Courtesy Rick Schwarz Collection.

Steamer *Gate City* aground near Moriches Inlet. Photo courtesy Steve Bielenda collection.

Hank Keatts with porthole recovered from the *Gate City* wreck. Photo by Carol Keatts.

Sketch of the *Gate City*. Drawn by Bill Willis.

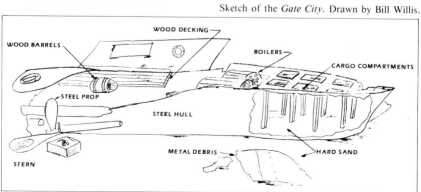

compound steam engine. She was owned by Ocean SS. Co., Savannah. The *Gate City* ran aground near Moriches Inlet in a dense fog and sank on February 8, 1900. Lifesavers on the beach used a breeches bouy to rescue all of her crew. At the time of her demise she was bound from Savannah, Georgia, to Boston with a cargo of cotton and molasses.

The interesting aspect of this wreck is that she was almost completely covered in sand until 1979, when a big winter storm opened up Moriches Inlet and uncovered her.

Today, the *Gate City* sits in 25 feet of water just east of Moriches Inlet.

G&D

This wreck has been unidentified for many years. She was originally found and named by a charter boat captain. He named the wreck after two girls that were on his boat that day, *Gloria and Doris*. The name stuck, and even today, nautical charts refer to the wreck as the *G&D*.

Jackie Nawrocky finds a porthole in the bow of the *G&D* wreck. Photo by Pete Nawrocky.

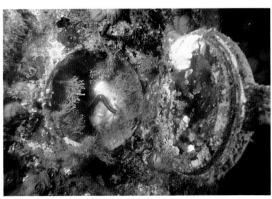

Porthole on the *G&D*. Photo by Pete Nawrocky.

Dan Berg on left and Jim D'Alessio with nine and eleven pound lobsters from the *G&D*.

In the original *Wreck Valley* book, I wrote that the *G&D Wreck* was most likely a vessel named *Durley Chine*. This assumption was proven wrong when diver, Rick Jaszyn, found a bell with the name *Durley Chine* on another previously unidentified wreck known as *Bacardi*. The true identity of the *G&D* wreck is still waiting for some lucky diver to find a piece of the puzzle that allows us to identify her.

This was the second shipwreck I dove after being certified over ten years ago. The very first descent produced an eleven pound lobster for my buddy Jim D'Alessio. On our second dive, I caught a nine pound bug moving into the same hole. Over the years I have been rewarded again and again by returning to this same spot on the wreck, which is a half circular hole in one of her boilers.

The *G&D* lies 14 miles out of Jones Inlet in 110 feet of water. Her boilers are still standing upright, her intact bow leaning on its side. Her beams and ribbing rise out of the sand, leaving no trace of the form they once held. The wreck is a haven for huge lobsters, cod, blackfish and ling. I have seen everything from giant ocean sunfish, dolphins, and turtles to seahorses at this site. For divers and fishermen alike, she is considered to be one of the best wrecks in the area.

GREAT ISAAC

The *Great Isaac* was a 185 foot long, 37 foot wide V-4 ocean going tug. She was built by General Ship and Engine Works, Boston, Massachusetts, in 1944 and was powered by twin diesel engines.

On April 16, 1947, while towing the Thomas M. Cooley, a liberty ship, from Norfolk, Virginia, to New York, and while passing through a dense fog bank, she was struck amidships on her port side by the Norwegian freighter, Bandeirante. Captain Ernest McCleary, and 27 of his crew abandoned ship and were lucky enough to be picked up by the Bandeirante. The *Great Isaac* was doomed and went down shortly after.

Today, the *Great Isaac* is a fantastic three dimensional shipwreck. Her totally intact remains rest on her port side and are buried so that only half of her hull rises above the sea bed. Depth at the wreck ranges from 85 to 90 feet. This wreck is often penetrated by experienced wreck divers looking for artifacts and lobsters. Just remember that due to the extreme angle at

The 185 foot long, 37 foot wide V-4 ocean going tug *Great Isaac*. Sketch © Charles P. Zimmaro 1990.

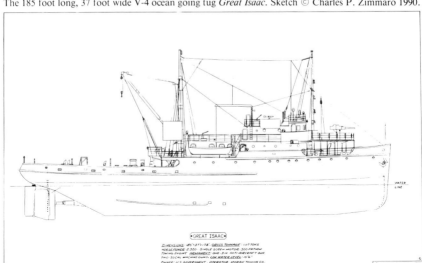

Chuck Zimmaro drew this beautiful detailed sketch of the *Great Isaac* on the bottom. © Charles P. Zimmaro 1990.

which this tug lies, it is easy to get disoriented. As always, a penetration line is recommended. Chuck Zimmaro drew a beautiful detailed sketch of this wreck on the bottom. His drawing allows divers who have never been on her to get a clear picture of how she rests before even getting wet.

GULFTRADE

The tanker, *Gulftrade*, was built in 1920 by Sun Building Co., Chester, Pennsylvania. She was 430 feet long, 59 feet wide and weighed 6,776 gross tons. The *Gulftrade* had been running blacked out in accordance with navy policy for avoiding U-Boats, but because there were other ships in the vicinity and in order to reduce the possibility of collision, her running lights were turned on. On March 10, 1942, under the command of Captain Torger Olsen, while en route from Port Arthur, Texas, to New York with a cargo of 80,000 gallons of fuel oil, a torpedo from the U-588 exploded amidships, breaking the tanker in two.

Fire filled the night sky. The Antietam, a Coast Guard vessel, rushed to her aid. Rescuers were able to pick up eight men including the Captain from one of her stern life boats. Unfortunately, the Antietam wasn't able to maneuver closer since a line had fouled in her propeller. On the still floating stern section remained seven men waiting for help. Two hours later, the seven where taken off by the Navy tender, Larch. Out of a total of 34 men, only 16 survived.

Today, the *Gulftrade* is actually two dive sites. The scattered bow section

The tanker *Gulftrade* sinking after being torpedoed in 1942. Photo courtesy National Archives.

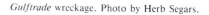

is resting in 60 feet of water, eight miles from Barnegat Inlet. The bow wreckage was blown up so as not to cause a hazard to navigation. The stern section drifted about ten miles before settling in deeper water of 90 feet, 13 miles from Barnegat Inlet. Her stern section was not left alone after sinking either, but was wire dragged clear to a depth of 50 feet for safe navigation.

HOWARD

In 1911, the steam tug, *Howard*, was trying to salvage copper ore from the *Roda* wreck which had sunk three years earlier. She arrived from New York and anchored offshore. During her first night out, a gale blew up, causing her to drag anchor and eventually she ended up aground. All nine crew members were rescued without mishap, but the *Howard* broke up in the surf.

Today, the *Howard*, also known as the *Scow Wreck*, lies one quarter of a mile southeast from the *Peter Rickmers Wreck*, up on the surf line in 25 feet of water.

HYLTON CASTLE

The British three-masted freight steamship, *Hylton Castle*, was built in

Sunderland, England, in 1871 by the Oswald and Co. ship builders. She was 251 feet long, 32 feet wide, displaced 1,258 gross tons, had seven water tight compartments and was owned by Surtees and Co., of North Shields.

On January 11, 1886, while bound from New York to Rouen with a cargo of 57,880 bushels of corn, the *Hylton Castle* got caught in a heavy gale. After a terrific beating, she literally began to break up. The crew abandoned her into two life boats with one containing nine men and the other 13. Within an hour, the big ship sank, bow first into the freezing ocean. One life boat managed to row ashore through the icy winter weather. Captain Colvin and his boat didn't have it as good. They broke three oars and ended up drifting for three days before being picked up by the fishing smack, Stephen Woolsey.

Today, the *Hylton Castle* lies eleven miles out from Fire Island Inlet in 95 feet of water. Her scattered wreckage is an excellent home for sea bass, blackfish, cod, ling and lobsters. Her propeller and engine are still recognizable.

IBERIA

The *Iberia*, an old tramp steamer, was owned by merchants in Marseilles,

Cunard liner Umbria colliding with the steamer *Iberia*. Courtesy Frank Litter.

Iberia

Iberia underwater. Photo courtesy Pete Nawrocky

France, and built in 1881 by the S and H Morton Co., in Leith, Scotland. She displaced 1,388 tons, was 255 feet long and 36 feet wide.

The *Iberia*, under the command of Captain Sagolis, was bound from the Persian Gulf to New York. She developed engine trouble just a few miles off Long Island, where she lay at anchor for three weeks awaiting repairs. On Saturday, November 10, 1888, the 520 foot long Cunard luxury liner, Umbria, bound for Liverpool, encountered dense fog. At 1:18 PM, the

Sketch of the *Iberia* on the bottom. Drawn by George Quirk and Dan Berg.

Dennis Lee Berg (left) and Dan Berg with crates recovered from the *Iberia*. Each crate end reads "Arnold Cheney & Co, Golden Dates, 158 Water St New York". Photo by Rick Schwarz.

Captain Frank Persico and bronze capstan cover from the *Iberia*. Photo by Daniel Berg.

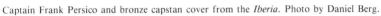

Iberia was spotted, steaming slowly into the path of the Umbria. Although engines were put into full reverse, the Umbria sliced off the stern of the ill-fated Fabre Line *Iberia*.

Both ships remained near each other at anchor overnight, but by the next morning, the *Iberia* was noticeably lower by the stern. Within hours, a bulkhead gave way, sending the *Iberia*, plus her cargo of dates, coffee and wool to rest in 60 feet of water.

The *Iberia's* bulkheads and sides have broken down, leaving ribs and wreckage scattered on the sand bottom. Divers can still find wood crates that once contained her cargo of dates or swim over a large four-bladed steel propeller. To the best of my knowledge, no one has ever located the missing stern overhang section, but her main wreckage lies midway between Jones and Debs Inlets about three miles offshore.

A few years back, Captain Frank Persico, recovered a bronze capstan cover from the *Iberia*. What made this artifact of particular interest to me was knowing that it was found in the open and that literally thousands of divers had to swim right over it before Frank's trained eyes recognized this prized artifact.

IMMACULATA

The *Immaculata* lies in 90 to 100 feet of water, 18 miles south of Jones Inlet. Said to be three old garbage barges sunk in the 1920s, this wreck, or wrecks, contains many old bottles buried in and around her broken remains.

When I first dove this wreck, I found small pieces of doll house furniture made of china and some ceramic bottles. Today, years later, the wreck is still producing artifacts for divers who explore her scattered ribs. There is also a large fluted anchor in an area of the wreck that appears to be the

Ceramic bottle from the *Immaculata*. Photo by Bill Campbell.

bow section. The bottom composition is very silty, so divers should make a conscious effort not to stir it up.

IOANNIS P. GOULANDRIS

The *Ioannis P. Goulandris*, sometimes referred to as the *Junior*, was built in 1910 by Craig Taylor & Co., Ltd., Stockton, England. Originally named *Maria Stathatos*, she was 362 feet long and 52 feet wide.

On December 1, 1942, the *Goulandris* was en route from Virginia, to Searsport, Maine. It was 10:30 PM and this ship as well as all other vessels in the area were running without navigation lights in an effort to make it harder for German U-Boats to find a target. Because of this strategy, collisions were always feared, and this night their fear turned into reality when the Panamanian freighter, Intrepido, rammed the *Goulandris*.

Ioannis P. Goulandris. Photo courtesy U.S. Coast Guard.

Helm from the *Goulandris* being lifted onto the dive boat. Photo by George Hoffman.

Fortunately, all of the 31 crew were rescued by the Intrepido, but the *Goulandris* slipped beneath the surface into the deep dark water known as the Mud Hole.

The *Ioannis P. Goulandris* now lies in 195 to 200 feet of water. She has remained completely intact but rests in an area known for its poor visibility. This wreck is too deep for sport divers but is visited on occasion by experienced deep divers.

IRMA C

The *Irma C*, an old coal barge, rests a few miles east of the *G&D* wreck. Her remains have been reduced to a small low-lying patch of wreckage, so that fishing or dive boats may find it a little tricky to anchor on her.

Once in the water, divers will usually find good visibility and an abundance of marine life on this wreck which rests in 105 feet of water. The way her ribs have spread out over time makes perfect homes for lobsters, which are abundant on this as well as other wrecks in the vicinity.

JOHN C. FITZPATRICK

Rare photograph of the *John C. Fitzpatrick*. Courtesy Dossin Museum, Detroit, Michigan.

Diver Ronald Barnes, from the Aquarians dive club, found the windlass cover that identified this wreck as the *Fitzpatrick*. Photo courtesy Bill deMarigny.

This previously unidentified wreck has been known as the *Jug* for years. Two years ago, Ron Barnes, of the Aquarians Dive Club, found and recovered her bronze windlass cover. Written on his artifact, Ron found the following information: "*John C. Fitzpatrick*, American Ship Windlass Co. Providence RI, 1892. F. W. Wheeler & Co. Shipbuilder, West Bay City, Michigan." Ron's find identified the wreck as the *John C. Fitzpatrick*, a fourmasted wooden schooner built in 1892. She was 242 feet long, had a 39 foot beam and 16 foot draft. The *Fitzpatrick* displaced 1,277 gross tons and 1,207 net tons.

On April 3, 1903, the *Fitzpatrick*, which had been converted to a barge, was being towed by the tugboat, Sweepstakes, from Philadelphia to New Bedford with 2400 tons of Bituminous coal. The Barge's boiler blew up and she sank immediately with her entire crew of five. At the time, the *Fitzpatrick* was owned by Boutelle Transportation Company of Cleveland, Ohio.

Today, the *John C. Fitzpatrick* lies scattered on the ocean floor in 130 to 140 feet of water out of Shinnecock inlet. Her remains are excellent for finding big lobsters.

KENOSHA

This wreck, which has always been known as the *Fire Island Lightship*, lies in 105 feet of water, ten miles southeast of Fire Island Inlet. Until 1986, she was still a mystery to us. Although a few sources report the *Lightship* sinking on May 8, 1916, she really didn't. On this date, the liner, Philadelphian, collided with the *Fire Island Lightship*, but although damaged, she was towed to Staten Island where full repairs were made.

"After diving this wreck and finding a wood hulled ship, I discovered and confirmed that this truly could not have been the steel hulled *Lightship*, but a wreck given the name for its location". This was taken from the original *Wreck Valley* book, but we now have discovered her true identity to be that of the *Kenosha*.

On August 13, 1986, aboard the Research Vessel Wahoo, a group of divers steamed toward the *Lightship*. After the first dive, Marc Weiss surfaced with the ship's brass windlass cover which turned out to be the key to identifying the wreck. Engraved on it were the words "*Madagascar*, James

The *Madagascar* would later change names and sail as *Kenosha*. Photo courtesy Dossin Great Lakes Museum, Detroit, Michigan.

For years the wreck we now know to be *Kenosha* had been referred to as the *Fire Island Lightship.* The original *Lightship* had been reported lost in many sources but it actuality had never sunk. Photo courtesy George Quirk.

Captain Steve Bielenda holds capstan cover that lead to identification of wreck. Photo by Daniel Berg.

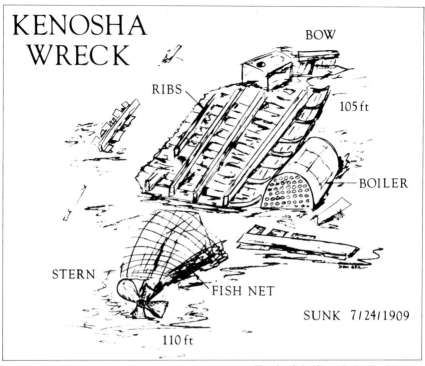

KENOSHA
WRECK

BOW

RIBS

105 ft

BOILER

STERN

FISH NET

SUNK 7/24/1909

110 ft

Sketch of the *Kenosha* by Daniel Berg.

Lobster tangled in monofilament line. Photo courtesy John Lachenmayer.

Lobsters from the *Kenosha*. Photo by Captain Steve Bielenda.

Author Dan Berg with thirteen and nine pound lobsters caught on the *Kenosha* in 1986. Photo by Steve Bielenda.

The author with a six pound lobster from the *Kenosha* in 1983. Photo by Rick Schwarz.

Harvey Leonard caught this 24 pound lobster in June 1983.

67

Davidson, American Shipbuilders Company.'' With this information, I started to research the wreck. Although all of my usual channels of information produced nothing on a vessel named *Madagascar* sinking off Long Island, I eventually discovered that the *Madagascar*, which was a 243 foot, wood hulled inland freighter built in 1894, had changed names in 1907 to *Kenosha*, before foundering on July 24, 1909. At the time of her sinking, she was carrying a cargo of coal and had twelve crew on board. It was not until October of 1989 that I was finally able to locate a topside photograph. We could see at last what this vessel had actually looked like.

The *Kenosha* is one of the best and my favorite lobstering wrecks in the area. Five pound lobsters are almost commonplace, and lobsters up to 15 pounds can still be seen by divers who look deep inside her crisscrossed ribs. But just because divers can see them, it doesn't mean they can catch them. It's like sticking your hand in a cookie jar and grabbing a big handful. You can easily put your hand on a big bug, but more often than not, you can't pull your hand out of the hole with a fistful of lobster.

LANA CAROL

This steel hulled, ocean going fishing vessel was built in 1973. She was 71 feet long, had a 21 foot beam and displaced 104 gross tons.

Lana Carol. Photo courtesy Pete Nawrocky.

Sketch of the *Lana Carol* drawn by Al Hofmann.

In October of 1976, the *Lana Carol* was dredging for scallops when she floundered, possibly due to the rough sea or maybe even from being overloaded. All four aboard were rescued before the fishing boat slipped beneath the surface.

Today, the wreck rests upright in 85 feet of water with rigging out. She comes up 20 feet off the bottom and makes a nice beginner to intermediate wreck dive. Her remains are very photogenic on good visibility days.

LILLIAN

The *Lillian* was built in 1920 by the Bethlehem Ship Building Company and was owned and operated by A.H. Bull Steam Ship Company. She had a 328 foot length and a 46 foot beam, displaced 3,482 tons and was powered by 292 nhp triple expansion engines.

On February 26, 1939, while hauling a cargo of sugar into New York, the *Lillian* ran into a heavy fog bank. At 6:53 PM, still enveloped in fog, Captain Frank Buyer saw another ship, the Wiegand, steaming directly toward him. Although both ships tried evasive maneuvers, it was too late.

Lillian

The 328 foot steamer *Lillian*. Photo courtesy Steamship Historical Society Collection, University of Baltimore Library.

Porthole on the *Lillian*. Photo by Brad Sheard.

Captain John Lachenmayer holds porthole from the *Lillian*. Photo by Dan Berg.

The *Lillian* rammed the Lloyd Line freighter on her starboard bow, giving her a twelve foot gash. This hole was above the water line and caused no immediate danger to the Wiegand. The *Lillian*, however, suffered greatly and almost immediately started to sink. Before abandoning ship, William Helmbold, the radio operator, locked his key to send a continuous SOS signal. This action not only helped the Coast Guard home in on the sinking vessel and rescue her 17 crew members but caused havoc on the radio waves for nearly eight hours. It seemed the *Lillian* was not ready to quickly settle into her watery grave. The vessel remained afloat with her radio automatically sending SOS signals. The Coast Guard finally had to shoot down her aerial to clear the radio waves. Ironically, after staying afloat for 18 hours after her collision, the *Lillian* finally sank when the salvage ship, Relief, had just come within sight.

The *Lillian* rests in 150 feet of water, 38 miles out of Debs Inlet. According to John Lachenmayer, this wreck is laid out similar to the *Iberia* only deeper. Her hull supports a wide array of life, including cod, ling and lobsters, while being in deep enough water to bring in sharks and, on occasion, giant tuna.

LINDA

The *Linda* is an unidentified wood wreck, most likely a schooner. She lies

Diver Pete Guglieri on the *Linda*. Photo by Brad Sheard.

20 miles out of Fire Island Inlet, about ten miles southwest of the *Oregon* wreck. She is sitting upright in 135 to 140 feet of water and is best known for the amount of dead eyes that have been recovered from her remains.

For years, many people have speculated that this wreck is actually the remains of the *Charles R. Morse*, the schooner that had left Baltimore for Boston with a cargo of coal on March 6, 1886, and was most likely the schooner that struck the *Oregon* on March 14. I have even seen articles that desperately try to connect the two by association of date and location. I for one am not convinced. In fact, although it is possible, I would expect an extreme amount of bow damage to a small wooden schooner that pierced through the huge steel hull of the *Oregon*. In fact, the NEW YORK TIMES reported that the "Coaster which had done all the damage drifted about in the neighborhood of the *Oregon* throughout the morning, her head gear all gone and her cutwater stove in." The bow of the *Linda* wreck is relatively intact. Only time will tell her true identity. Someone will surely find an artifact that will allow us to settle this debate once and for all. Recently, two divers have come close. Tony Bliss found and recovered the ship's bell a few years back, but unfortunately it didn't bear any name or marking that would help us in identification. George Quirk found her compass which was still mounted into a gimbel and had calibration dates. This may help in identifying her, but further investigation and information is needed.

LIZZIE D

A tug weighing 122 gross tons, the *Lizzie D* was 15 years old and valued at $25,000 when she sunk on October 19, 1922.

According to the owner's casualty report, filed with the Department of

Rare photograph of the *Lizzie D*. Courtesy Steve Bielenda Collection.

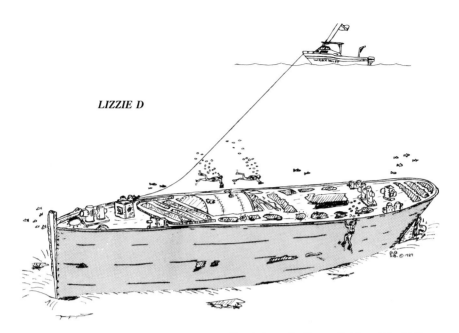

LIZZIE D

The *Lizzie* as she rests today in 80 feet of water. Sketch drawn by George Quirk and Daniel Berg.

Commerce's Bureau of Navigation, the 84 foot tug was on a "cruise of the narrows," carrying no cargo, but with eight crew members on board when she went down. The *Lizzie D* was reported sunk due to unknown reasons. All of her crew were lost.

In July of 1977, captain John Larsen located the wreck. He discovered that this was not just a sunken tug boat, but a prohibition rum runner. Joan Fullmur recovered the ship's brass bell which identified the wreck. Also recovered were portholes and crates full of 100 proof Kentucky bourbon and Canadian rye whiskey. This first group of divers on the *Lizzie* reported that the whiskey "still smelled good". Immediately after, divers from all over started to reap the bounty from this site. Her bronze helm was soon found 50 feet away, lying in the sand off her starboard bow.

As a side note, ever since I was first certified and started diving local shipwrecks, I was always under the assumption that a diver who found one, two or at the most three bottles on this wreck during any dive was extremely lucky. Well, two summers ago Bill Campbell, Rick Schwarz, Steve Jonassen and I were extremely lucky. In one day we recovered almost 40 bottles. Steve found a complete case of dark green "Johnny Walker" bottles; Bill found an assortment including one full bourbon bottle which still had a lead seal over the cork. This seal read "Bourbon Whiskey 100 proof". Rick and

Lizzie D

A diver explorers the *Lizzie D's* stern. Photo courtesy Jozef Koppelman.

Ladder leading to *Lizzie's* deck. Photo by Peter Nawrocky.

Diver Joan Fullmur and the bell she recovered from the *Lizzie D*. Photo courtesy Steve Bielenda collection.

The author, Dan Berg, displays
prohibition whiskey bottles
recovered in 1987. Photo by
Rick Schwarz.

Bill Campbell with a full
bourbon bottle he found in 1988.
Photo by Dan Berg.

I also filled our bug bags and had four bourbon bottles still containing whiskey. Not a bad catch for a day's diving!.

Since that day, we have returned to the wreck many times. Our artifacts have been displayed in local museums, libraries, and in the windows of local dive shops. Some of the bottles and underwater video taken that day have even appeared on local cable TV shows. But best of all, we now know that the *Lizzie D*, is still delivering her cargo of illegal whiskey, not to the "speak easy's" of the roaring 20's, but to a few lucky sport divers who frequent an area known as *Wreck Valley*.

Today, the *Rum Runner,* as she is more commonly known, rests in 80 feet of water, eight miles southeast of Atlantic Beach Inlet. Her hull sits upright and mostly intact except for the entire upper deck which lies in pieces surrounding the wreck. She looks like a giant rowboat with many openings in the main deck. Her boiler rises just over her deck and openings ahead and astern allow easy penetration. Most of the cargo of full bottles is gone; her interior is littered with about two feet of broken glass and mud, but for the lucky few who dig in and around the wreck, intact bottles can still be found. If a diver is lucky enough to find an unbroken bottle, it is usually empty with the cork forced inside the glass. Increasing ambient pressure during the sinking compressed the small amount of air in a full bottle, causing the cork to be sucked inward. Bourbon bottles seem to hold their corks the best due to the shape of the bottle's neck. Therefore, whenever a bourbon bottle is found, the chances are much greater that it may still contain whiskey. Fishermen can hit the *Rum Runner* on their way to or from almost any of the west end's deep fishing grounds.

MARGARET

The *Margaret* is an unknown shipwreck, said to be that of a tug boat. She sits only one mile south of Deb's Inlet in 40 feet of water.

In 1985, when I dove this wreck, visibility was so bad that I couldn't even see what my hand was touching. I did feel a lot of steel cable draped over what appeared to be a hand railing. Because of her location, which is so close to the mouth of Deb's Inlet, a strong current, which kicks up sediment and reduces visibility is usually present making the wreck inaccessible, or at least undesirable for divers. I have, however, seen many charter fishing boats anchored over the *Margaret* and have heard that if you don't mind losing some lead sinkers, fishing for blackfish on the *Margaret* can be quite productive.

MAURICE TRACY

The *Maurice Tracy* was a 253 foot by 43 foot, steam powered collier. Built back in 1916, she was originally named *Nordstrand* and later *Sekstant*.

On June 17, 1944, the *Maurice Tracy* was en route from Portland, Maine, to Norfolk, Virginia, with a cargo of coal, when she was rammed by the liberty ship, Jesse Billingsley. The *Tracy's* crew were all rescued from the slow sinking vessel by the sub chaser, SC-412, which along with the SC-1355 had been escorting the Jesse Billingsley.

Maurice Tracy. Photo courtesy U.S. Coast Guard.

Today, the wreck sits in 70 feet of water. Most of her hull plates and structure have become a low lying debris field. This wreck is a good spot for lobsters.

MISTLETOE

Also known as the *East Wreck*, the *Mistletoe* was a wood hulled side wheel steam ship built in Chester, Pennsylvania, in 1872. She was 152.6 feet long by 26.7 feet wide, displaced 362 gross tons and was powered by a 370 horsepower engine.

On May 5, 1924, while bound for an offshore fishing ground under the command of Captain Dan Gully and carrying 74 passengers and ten crew members, she caught fire, burned to the water line and sank a few miles off

Mistletoe

Wood hulled side wheel steamship *Mistletoe*. Courtesy Steamship Historical Society Collection, University of Baltimore Library.

Mistletoe sketch by Dan Berg.

MISTLETOE SUNK 1924

Diver Jim D'Alessio with a twelve pound blackfish he speared on the *Mistletoe* wreck. Photo by Dan Berg.

Far Rockaway. It may never be known what caused the fire that day, but all on board where fortunate to be transferred to small fishing boats that had come to lend aid. Luckily, no lives were lost.

After examining two photocopies copies of an old newspaper article, given to me by Captain Bill Reddan, I came across a couple of interesting facts. One of the photographs in the article shows the *Mistletoe* with excursion passengers on her upper deck waiting for rescue boats. In this picture you can see that she is flying the American flag upside down, a signal of distress. The other photograph shows the pilot boat, *Sandy Hook*, which would herself sink in 1939, in the foreground standing by to lend assistance.

The *Mistletoe* now lies in 42 feet of water, four miles southwest of East Rockaway Inlet. Her remains provide homes for lobster, ling, blackfish and even small cod. Divers can see the remains of her paddle wheels and boilers as well as lots of copper sheeting. The copper sheeting had been used to plate her hull so worms couldn't eat through the wood.

MOHAWK

The Ward Line cruise ship, *Mohawk*, was built in October, 1926, at

79

Mohawk

The Ward Line cruise ship *Mohawk* was sunk by collision on January 24, 1935. Photo courtesy Steamship Historical Society Collection, University of Baltimore Library.

A porthole wedged between debris on the *Mohawk* wreck. Photo courtesy Pete Nawrocky.

Newport News Ship Building & Drydock Co. She was 387.5 feet long, 54.3 feet wide, had 4,200 ihp turbine engines and displaced 5,896 gross tons.

Under the command of Captain J.E. Wood, the *Mohawk* left New York on January 24, 1935. She was carrying 53 passengers, 110 crew members and a general cargo. Shortly after leaving port, and within one eighth of a mile of the freighter, Talisman, the *Mohawk's* automatic steering device went haywire. At the time, she was steaming at her full speed of 14 knots. Although this alone would not explain why the Norwegian freighter, Talisman, smashed through her port side, some say the *Mohawk's* lights also failed. Almost immediately after the collision the *Mohawk* started to list heavily to her port side. At least two survivors report they saw Captain J.E. Wood still on the bridge of the sinking ship during her last moments. Within an hour she was on the bottom, leaving her survivors to endure the bitter cold water.

The rescue ships, Algonquin and Limon, picked up a total of six life boats with just over 100 survivors. A total of 46 people were killed, 16 passengers and 30 crew, mostly due to exposure to the near freezing temperature.

In July of 1935, for navigational reasons the Army Corp's of Engineers blasted and wire dragged the wreck to a depth of 50 feet.

Today, the *Mohawk* lies in 80 feet of water, eight miles east of Manasquan Inlet. Her structure rises 20 feet off the bottom and supplies a home for all kinds of aquatic life.

R.C. MOHAWK

The *Revenue Cutter, Mohawk*, was built in 1902 in Richmond, Virginia. She was commissioned on May 10, 1904, and was owned by the Treasury Department. The *Mohawk* was 205 feet, six inches long, 32 feet wide, powered by steam and displaced 980 tons. On April 6, 1917, she was temporarily transferred to the Navy. The *Mohawk* served coastal duty for convoy operations.

On October 1, 1917, the single screw cutter was sunk due to a collision with the British tanker, SS Vennacher. According to the Navy's report of the incident, "The British vessel struck the *Mohawk* nearly at right angles, her stem cutting into the side amidships, abreast the engine room, between the launch davits, smashing the surf boat and cutting into the ship's side to such an extent that the use of a collision mat was out of the question. . . . Pumps

R.C. Mohawk

Revenue Cutter, Mohawk, was sunk due to collision on October 1, 1917. Photo courtesy Society for the Preservation of New England Antiquities, Boston Mass.

Revenue Cutter, Mohawk as she sits today in 100 feet of water. Sketch was drawn by George Quirk and Daniel Berg.

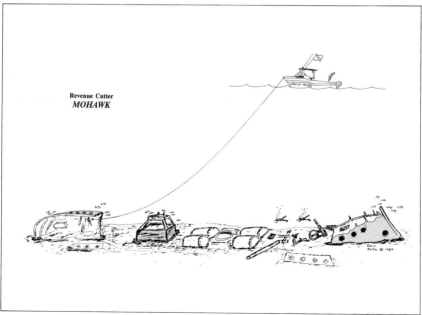

Diver Billy deMarigny and the stern helm he recovered from the *R.C. Mohawk*. Photo courtesy Aquarians Dive Club.

Brass builders plaque recovered by Bill deMarigny. Photo courtesy George Hoffman.

R.C. Mohawk

Bell Billy deMarigny recovered from the
R.C. Mohawk. Photo by Dan Berg.

Brass calendar George Quirk found on the
wreck. Photo by George Quirk.

Telegraph from the *Mohawk*.
Courtesy Bill deMarigny.

Two different style portholes,
china dish and a gauge
recovered in one dive by
Frank Persico.

R.C. Mohawk. Photo courtesy Mariners Museum, Newport News, Virginia.

were started at once, the general alarm sounded and all hands called to take stations for abandoning ship". The ship filled rapidly and began settling by the stern. She took one hour to go down which left plenty of time for all 77 crew members to be rescued by the USS Mohigan and USS Sabalo. The USS Bridge arrived on the scene and attached a cable to the *Mohawk's* bow bit. She then attempted to tow the *Mohawk* into shallow water. Before rescuers were able to generate any forward movement, it was noticed that the *Mohawk* had begun to sink rapidly and list heavily to port. The commanding officer of the Bridge was forced to cut the tow line and throw both engines into full speed ahead to get clear." With her bow high in the air, the *Mohawk* settled slowly emitting quantities of smoke".

Today, the *R.C. Mohawk* rests on a silty bottom, ten miles south of Debs Inlet, 12.5 miles from Sandy Hook in 100 feet of water. Her bow sits upright, amidships is broken down. Her boilers are recognizable, while her engine remains upright and her stern lies on its starboard side. For many years, her location was not too suitable for divers or fishermen, since it was almost directly under a sewage dump location, but this is changing with the new offshore dumping laws. In fact, the wreck has been cleaning up, visibility is better, and the bottom is becoming less silty. Just as an example, I have made many visits to this wreck over the past few years and have never until this year had more than two feet of visibility. On two trips this year, I've seen visibility upwards of 15 feet. As a side note, I would still not recommend eating any lobsters from this site due to the previous years of dumping, but she is definitely recommended to divers looking for artifacts.

OCEAN PRINCE

Floating *Dry Dock No. 4* was a 200 foot long, 85 foot wide and 35 foot high wooden barge. She was donated by New York Shipyards to be sunk as a fish haven off Fire Island. Before the *Dry Dock* was sunk, a variance was obtained from the Army Corp's of Engineers. This was necessary because the *Dry Dock* had such a high silhouette that she would stick above the minimum 50 foot clearance necessary for any material deposited on the reef.

On Saturday November 29, 1986, due to the efforts of Chet Zawacki, Captain Steve Bielenda, and the Captree Boatman's Association, *Dry Dock No. 4* completed her 14 hour tow from Jersey City to a predetermined location on the southeast corner of the Fire Island Artificial Reef. Her seacocks were opened at 9:30 AM, and within a half hour she had slipped beneath the waves.

Dry Dock #4, nick-named *Ocean Prince*, being towed from New Jersey to Fire Island. Courtesy Chet Zawacki.

The *Ocean Prince* sinking. Photo courtesy Chet Zawacki.

Dry Dock No. 4, nick-named *Ocean Prince* by Steve Bielenda after the tug boat who towed her, is now sitting in 71 feet of water. Her "V" shaped structure has broken down allowing lobsters, ling and blackfish to inhabit her twisted remains.

OREGON

The steamer *Oregon* was built for the Guion Line by John Elders Fairfield & Company of Glasgow, Scotland; in 1881. She was 518 feet long, had a beam of 54 feet and displaced 7,500 tons. She was powered by a three cylinder engine which put out upwards of 12,000 horsepower. Steam was generated by nine boilers, each almost 18 feet long, consuming a total of almost 240 tons of coal a day. Her modified clipper designed hull carried two enormous smoke stacks and was also fitted with four masts fully rigged for sail. The *Oregon* was one of the biggest and fastest ships of her time. Her interior was fitted and furnished with elaborate and costly materials. She had accommodations for 340 first class, 92 second class and 1110 steerage class passengers. She was also equipped with water tight compartments. The *Oregon* even had the distinction of making a record Trans-Atlantic crossing on her maiden voyage, claiming the coveted Blue-Riband award with a six day, ten hour and 40 minute crossing. The *Oregon*

Steamer *Oregon* had the distinction of making a record Trans-Atlantic crossing on her maiden voyage. Photo courtesy Steamship Historical Society Collection, University of Baltimore Library.

Oregon

The *Oregon*. Photo courtesy Steamship Historical Society Collection, University of Baltimore Library.

had sailed from Queenstown on October 7, 1883, and arrived in Sandy Hook just 7 days, 8 hours and 33 minutes later, averaging almost eighteen knots. This record was held until August of 1885.

In 1884, Stephen Guion went bankrupt. He sold the *Oregon* to his competitor, the Cunard Line, for 616,000 pounds.

On March 6, 1886, the *Oregon* departed Liverpool and steamed for New York. At 4:30 AM on March 14, 1886, only five miles off Fire Island N.Y., the *Oregon* was struck on her port side by a deep laden three masted schooner. The two vessels then drifted apart in the dark. Passengers on board the *Oregon* could hear the despairing cries of the schooner's crew as she foundered. The unknown schooner sank shortly after with all hands. Although no one has ever located the schooner, she is presumed to be the *Charles R. Morse* of Maine which was reported missing that night. None of the *Morse's* nine crew or any of her wreckage has ever been found, but the masts of a schooner were seen poking through the ocean's surface 16.5 miles east of the *Oregon* wreck.

John Hopkins, told NEW YORK TIMES reporters the following story. "I was the only passenger up. I had been sick all through the voyage and could not sleep. I was taking some toast and tea, when I heard a crash and felt a shock that shook the *Oregon* from end to end". "A frightful crash and clatter as of the falling of an immense mass of iron plates came from the port side". Another passenger stated that it was a clear calm night and

The *Oregon* managed to stay afloat for eight hours after the collision. This was time enough for all passengers and crew to be rescued. Courtesy Steve Bielenda collection.

After her sinking, much was questioned about how a Cunard Liner could possibly collide with a schooner on a clear night with a smooth sea. Photo courtesy Steve Bielenda.

Oregon

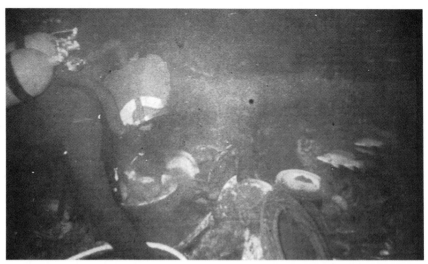

Mike DeCamp took this photograph when divers had first visited the *Oregon*. Note the abundance of china and portholes that literally covered the bottom.

he had seen the lights of an on coming ship for a half hour before the collision.

The *Oregon* had suffered a devastating wound but managed to stay afloat for eight hours after the collision. This was time enough for all 845 passengers and crew to be rescued by the schooner Fannie A. Gorhan, North German Loyd Steamship, Fulda, and the pilot boat, Phantom. Captain Cuttier was the last to leave his ship before she went bow first to the bottom. His comment to reporters was that "I never expected to see such an affair go off so easily". The sinking, however, didn't end without a heroic story or two. One hero was Officer Huston, who not only attempted to plug the huge hole in *Oregon's* hull with a makeshift canvas matt, which succeeded in delaying her sinking. He was also credited with saving at least three lives, two of which were children who fell in while being transferred to a lifeboat. "Huston plunged into the water at once and saved them". The TIMES reported that "not a soul on board was lost" and that three dogs, a terrier, a bull and a skye were also saved. The *Oregon* landed upright on the ocean floor with her masts poking through the surface.

After her sinking, much was questioned about how a Cunard Liner could possibly collide with a schooner on a clear night with a smooth sea, not to mention all the best navigational equipment. The MARINE JOURNAL, an American magazine, asked pertinent questions like "why were night glasses, which are provided to scan the horizon not used?. . . . Why was the *Oregon's* commanding officer below deck when his ship was in sight of land

Diver Dennis Kessler by
Steering Quadrant in
the *Oregon's* stern. Photo
by Brad Sheard.

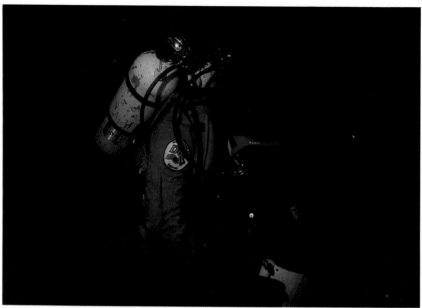

Dan Berg digs for china on the *Oregon* wreck. Photo by Bill Campbell.

China and silverware found on the *Oregon*. Courtesy Steve Bielenda.

Steve Bielenda with a china dish found on the *Oregon*. Photo by Hank Keatts.

Captain Steve Bielenda putting a
21 pound lobster into his bug bag.
Photo by Hank Keatts.

Diver Rick Schwarz with an intact
chamber pot he recovered from an
area just ahead of the boilers.
Photo by Dan Berg.

Oregon

Diver Rick Schwarz found this china dolls head while digging for china in 1988. Photo by Dan Berg.

Diver Craig Stemitez with a porthole from the *Oregon*. Photo courtesy Steve Bielenda.

This Dead Eye was found and recovered by Captain John Lachenmayer.

Oregon china. Photo by Steve Bielenda.

Oregon silverware. Photo by Steve Bielenda.

and in the track of vessel?''. The Journals last comment about the sinking ''We had hoped, however, to be spared that stale statement that 'The Captain was the last to leave the ship' who should be the last to leave - the cook?'' Many placed the blame on gross carelessness on the part of the *Oregon's* officers. Captain Cottlier was in his cabin asleep at the time of the accident, and his statement that the schooner had a white light visible is contradicted by at least one passenger, Mrs Hurst, who says that she saw a red light prior to the collision. Knowing which color light was visible is extremely important because it would allow investigators to determine which vessel had the right of way and which vessel was at fault. The answer was never learned. Although there was a hearing by a board of inquiry in Liverpool, passengers were not permitted to testify. The panel concluded that no blame could be placed on the officers of the *Oregon*. However, Captain Cottlier, the youngest skipper in Cunard's service, was discharged and no longer could the Cunard Line boast of never having lost a ship.

Merritt Chapman dispatched a crew of divers to the wreck in order to determine the possibility of salvage. The divers descended then returned to report that the *Oregon* was already broken in two, between hatches No. 2 and 3. ''The after part of the hull had been twisted out of line from the forward part showing that the vessel had sheered over as she went down and had then broken.'' There was no chance of raising her.

Today the *Oregon* lies in 125 to 130 feet of water, 21 miles south east of Fire Island Inlet. Her sides have given way, leaving only her engine standing

This sketch, by Steve Bielenda, shows the *Oregon* in her present condition.

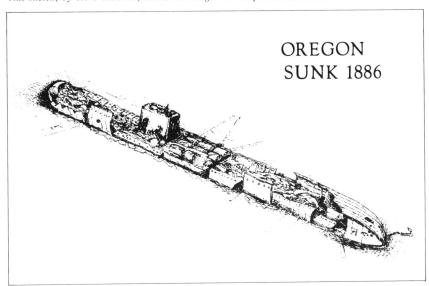

OREGON
SUNK 1886

upright. Divers have brought up all kinds of artifacts including portholes, ornate chandeliers and fine china stamped with the Cunard or Guion steamship crest. The *Oregon* is also well known for the abundance of lobsters, some as large as 20 pounds.

On March 14, 1986, I joined a group of divers lead by Captain Steve Bielenda aboard the R.V. Wahoo. We participated in a 100th anniversary commemorative dive on this magnificent shipwreck. The *Oregon* is one of the most spectacular wrecks on the east coast and is one of my favorite wrecks to dive.

PANTHER

The *Panther* was an ocean going tug, which was towing two barges when she encountered gale force winds. It was August 23, 1893, when the *Panther* with 20 crew members on board was en route from Boston to Philadelphia.

Al Bohem caught both of these huge lobsters on the *Panther*. One is 21 pounds and the other is 16 pounds. Photo courtesy Steve Bielenda.

In tow were the barges Lykens Valley and Victor. According to a survivor and as reported in the NEW YORK TIMES, the *Panther* "sprang a leak in the big storm. . . . She filled so rapidly that there was no hope of saving her. . . . The crew of 20 barely had time to adjust life preservers when she sank". Another survivor reported the following saga in his report to TIMES reporters: "After we had all climbed into the rigging the seas kept coming mountain high, sweeping clean over the boat. It took the men off the rigging like flies."

Today, the *Panther* sits in 55 to 60 feet of water, four miles out of Shinnecock Inlet. She lies on a sand bottom with her propeller, steam engine and boiler all resting in a straight line.

PATRICE McALLISTER

This 94 foot steel hulled tug boat was built in 1919 at Johnson Iron Works and was owned by McAllister Brothers Inc. She had at least three previous names including *M & T Tracy, Major Frazer* and *Degrey*.

On October 4, 1976, the *Patrice McAllister* was in tow by the Judith McAllister. They were en route from Camden, New Jersey, to Jersey City, where the *Patrice* would undergo a much needed engine overhaul. Unfortunately, they would never make it to port. The wind picked up and

These artifacts, which include her helm, compass, and lanterns, were recovered by the first divers to dive the *Patrice McAllister*. Photo courtesy George Hoffman.

the sea became too rough for the *Patrice* to handle. She slipped beneath the waves. John Bedon, captain of the Judith McAllister, was still attached to the wreck by his towing line. He stayed directly over her until the Coast Guard was able to bouy the location.

Today, the *Patrice McAllister* is sitting upright and intact in 55 feet of water. She makes an excellent intact wreck for divers to explore and enjoy.

PAULINE MARIE

The *Pauline Marie* was built by Sturgeon Bay Ship Building in 1943. She was an AK class freighter, 165 feet long and 32 feet wide.

The *Pauline Marie* starts to sink immediately after three explosions ripped several holes through her hull. Photo courtesy Bill Figely.

The *Pauline Marie* dives bow first to begin her new life as an artifical reef. Photo courtesy Bill Figely.

In 1985, the *Pauline Marie* was donated by Sea Coast Products to the New Jersey Fish, Game and Wildlife artificial reef program. The freighter was towed offshore, and on March 29, 1985, three charges were set in the vessel's hull, exploding and opening up several two foot holes below the water line. The *Pauline Marie* was sent downward to begin her new life as a fish haven.

Today, the *Pauline Marie* sits in 90 feet of water. She is a prime example of the benefits that marine life can gain from a three dimensional structure.

H.M.S. PENTLAND FIRTH

The *H.M.S. Pentland Firth* was a 164.4 foot by 27.4 foot British Patrol Boat. She was built in November, 1934, by the Cook, Wellington & Gemmel Co. Ship Builders in Beverly, England, and was originally owned by the Firth Steam Trawling Company Co. In 1939, she was purchased by the Royal Navy.

On September 19, 1942, she was performing convoy duty on loan to the American Navy when she was struck by the minesweeper, USS Chaffinch, and sunk a few miles west of Ambrose Light Tower. The wreck was determined to be a hazard to navigation and was quickly wire dragged clear to a depth of 50 feet.

Sketch of the *H.M.S. Pentland Firth.* Courtesy Frank Litter.

Today, The *Pentland Firth* lies in 70 feet of water, almost directly under the main shipping lanes within the Pilot's Triangle west of Ambrose Light Tower. She is low lying, and her steel plates overlap making good homes for lobster.

PERSEPHONE

The *Persephone* was a 468 foot long by 63.2 foot wide tanker, owned by the Panama Transport Company. She was built by Fried. Krupp Germaniawerft Act. Ges. in Germany and displaced 8,426 gross tons.

On May 25, 1942, while en route from Aruba to New York, travelling in convoy with a cargo of 90,000 barrels of fuel oil under the command of Captain Helge Quistgaard, she was struck in the stern by two German torpedoes fired from the U-593. The tanker sank stern first, taking nine of her 37 crew to a watery grave. Captain Quistgaard was the last to abandon

This photo was taken shortly after the *Persephone* was torpedoed. In fact two life rafts filled with survivors are visible in the photo. One is directly under the Navy blimp and the second is just ahead of her forward mast. Photo courtesy National Archives.

ship. He did so only after gathering all of his navigational equipment. The Captain, after being picked up by a Coast Guard vessel, requested and was returned to the wreck's bow where he recovered 23 bags of U.S. mail. Since the depth of water at this site is relatively shallow, her bow was able to stay above water even after her stern had become fully embedded in the ocean floor.

A salvage operation separated the *Persephone's* bow from her demolished sunken stern and towed it to New York. Almost 20,000 barrels of oil were recovered.

This was not the end of the story. The bow of the *Persephone* was eventually towed to Baltimore where it was fitted to the stern of the Esso tanker, Livingston Roe. The Roe's bow had been severely damaged by fire, but after some time in the shipyards and a new bow section from the *Persephone*, she was able to sail again.

The wreck of the *Persephone's* stern is now a scattered junk heap sitting in 55 feet of water, three miles out of Barnegat Inlet. The wreck is good for lobsters, blackfish and sea bass.

PETER RICKMERS

The four-masted bark *Peter Rickmers* aground at Short Beach. Photo Dan Berg collection.

Peter Rickmers

The *Peter Rickmers* was pounded by storm after storm until she was a total wreck. Photo courtesy South Street Seaport Museum, New York, N.Y.

The four-masted bark, *Peter Rickmers*, was built in Port Glasgow, Scotland in 1889. She was designated as a four-masted bark in England, but was classified as "fully rigged" in the United States. She was 2,958 gross tons and considered to be one of the finest and largest vessels of her kind.

On April 30, 1908, under the command of Captain Bachmann while en route from Perth Amboy, New Jersey, to Rangoon, Burmah , with 120,000 cases of kerosene and crude oil, she was caught in a heavy southeast gale. The wind and sea drove her hard aground near Short Beach. Due to the treacherous surf, lifesavers from Zachs Inlet, Short Beach and Point Lookout failed to get a boat to her. A message was sent, and the *R.C. Mohawk*, a vessel which would herself sink in 1917 plus two tug boats came from Sandy Hook to try their hand at pulling her off the bar. Their efforts failed. A final attempt was made to lighten her by throwing over some of the cargo, but this was too little too late. All crew members were finally brought ashore, but Captain George Bachmann stayed aboard with 40 wreckers who had boarded to try to save her precious cargo. The wreckers stayed aboard during storm after storm. Finally on May 15, in fear for their lives, they were safely brought to shore in breeches buoys by the lifesavers.

Today, the *Oil Wreck*, as she is sometimes called, sits in 15 to 20 feet of water completely buried beneath sand, one mile east of Jones Inlet.

The Dutch freighter *Pinta*. Courtesy Steve Bielenda collection.

PINTA

The *Pinta* was a 194 foot by 31 foot, 500 ton Dutch freighter. She was built in 1959 by N.V. Bodewes, and was owned by Dammers & Vanderheids Shipping and Trading Company, located in the Netherlands.

On May 8, 1963, while inbound from Central America, carrying a cargo of lumber, she was struck broadside on her port side by the British freighter, SS City of Perth. The *Pinta* remained afloat for only 48 minutes while all twelve of her crew including Captain Korpelshoek took to a life boat. All were safely picked up by the City of Perth.

The collision was never investigated because it involved two foreign vessels in international water. To date, we don't really know who was at fault or how two modern vessels with radar could have collided on a clear calm day.

Today, the *Pinta* lies in 85 to 90 feet of water, eight miles from Shark River Inlet and 22 miles out of Debs Inlet. She rests on her port side and is still almost completely intact. Her masts and boom are lying in the sand. Her cargo holds are open and her cargo of wood is now a favorite area for divers in search of lobsters.

Pinta

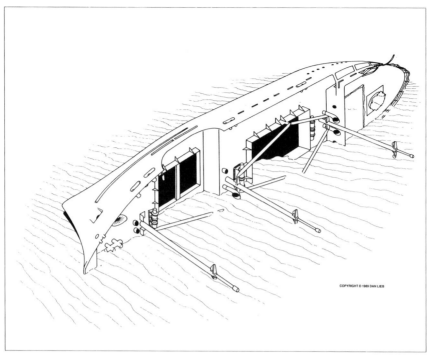

Today, the *Pinta* lies in 85 to 90 feet of water. She is resting on her port side and is still completely intact. Sketch © Dan Lieb 1989.

Hull side view of the *Pinta*. Sketch © Dan Lieb 1989.

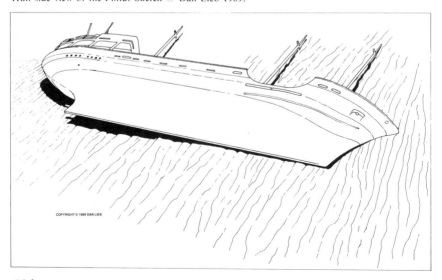

Mike DeCamp was one of the first divers to descend on the *Pinta* after her collision in 1963. He took this photograph of her stern with her name still legible. Photo courtesy Mike DeCamp.

Diver with the *Pinta's* bell. Photo courtesy Paul J. Tzimoulis.

PIPE BARGE

The *Pipe Barge* is a wreck of a push barge located just inshore of the Atlantic Beach Fish Haven. The *Pipe Barge*, as the name implies, had been transporting pipe when she sunk. The actual history and cause of her sinking is unknown, but that doesn't change the fact that she has produced many lobsters over the years, especially on night dives.

The *Pipe Barge* sits in 60 feet of water and remains mostly intact. She sits upright on a sand bottom and her bow section can be entered through an opening on her starboard side. Lobsters inhabit many of the pipes and holes in and around the wreck, but I always make a point of looking in a large pipe located in the sand off her port side. This is a favorite home for larger lobsters.

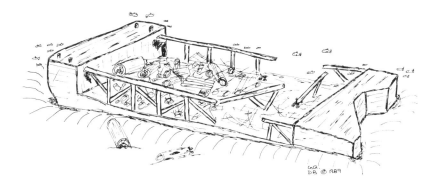

The *Pipe Barge*. By Dan Berg and George Quirk.

PRINCESS ANNE

The *Princess Anne* was built in Chester, Pennsylvania. Constructed in 1897 for the Old Dominion Line, the single screw steam ship was 350 feet long by 42 feet wide and had a displacement of 3,629 gross tons.

On February 6, 1930, with 74 crew members and 32 passengers on board, Captain Frank Seay missed the entrance to New York Harbor and stranded his ship on Rockaway Shoals. At 2:00 AM, the stranded ship was seen from the Life Saving Service watchtower at Rockaway Point. Because of severe weather and six foot snow drifts, it was impossible for anyone to reach her immediately. At 5:00 AM the next morning, a life boat was finally able to heave its way through the somewhat reduced surf; it succeeded in taking all passengers to safety. The crew, however, refused to leave without their luggage which could not fit in the life boat.

On February 15, nine days after she ran aground, the ship, still carrying 74

Princess Anne

The steamship *Princess Anne*. Courtesy Frank Persico collection.

The *Princess Anne* broke up soon after running aground. Photo courtesy South Street Seaport Museum, New York, N.Y.

Wreck of the *Princess Anne*. Dan Berg collection.

stubborn crew members, started to break apart. Rivets popped and steel plates slid into the sea. With this, the crew raised a distress signal and were hauled to safety. Later that day, the big ship broke into two.

Although the *Princess Anne* protruded from the water for many years, constant pounding of the sea and shifting sands have all but buried her under Rockaway Beach. The wreck, which most people refer to as the *Princess Anne*, is really an unidentified wood wreck which sits in 20 feet of water just east of Rockaway Point.

RASCAL

The *Rascal*, an ex-government boat, was a 41 foot, single screw, charter boat powered by a 671 diesel engine. Her owner and captain was the late Louis Schroeder, who passed away in the Fall of 1985. Mr. Schroeder, who was a devoted scuba diver since the early 1960's, also owned the Wheel House dive shop. His favorite ship wreck was the paddle wheeler, *Black Warrior*, which was sunk in 1859.

On November 17, 1985, as a memorial to captain Louis Schroeder, the *Rascal* was sunk just east of the *Black Warrior* in 40 feet of water.

REGGIE

The *Reggie* is rumored to be the remains of a barge. The wreck is located in 105 feet of water off Fire Island and is one of the best lobster wrecks in the area. I have only had the pleasure of visiting this wreck about four times. In my opinion the story about this wreck being a barge is inaccurate. She definitely needs more extensive exploration.

The *Reggie's* steel hulled pointed bow is lying upside down. Everything behind her bow is scattered in a low lying debris field. On my dive trips to the wreck, I have not seen any sign of machinery or rigging, but have located a capstan buried under her bow.

Diver Steve Jonassen (left) and Bill Campbell with lobster and ling from the wreck of the *Reggie*. Photo by Dan Berg.

RELIEF SHIP (WAL-505)

The *Relief Ship* was built by the New York Shipbuilding Company, Camden, New Jersey, in 1904. She was 129 feet long by 28.6 feet wide. She had a displacement of 566 tons and was powered by 600 horsepower diesel engine which was built by General Motors. The *Lightship* also carried a 60,000 candle power oscillating light, one of the most powerful lights of its kind in the world.

The *Relief Lightship's* beacons were flashing and her foghorn was sounding when she was struck by the freighter Green Bay. Photo Courtesy South Street Seaport Museum, New York, N.Y.

The author made this sketch of the *Relief Ship* in 1984.

RELIEF SHIP
SUNK
JUNE 24 1960

Al Catalfumo recovered this 6,000 pound light mast from the wreck in 1976.

Brass door lock and keys from the *Relief Ship* radio room. Recovered and photographed by George Quirk.

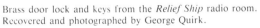

On June 24, 1960, the red hulled, white lettered *Relief Lightship* was on station filling in for the Wal-613 which was in Staten Island for her yearly overhaul. The *Wal-505's* beacons were flashing and her foghorn was sounding at regular intervals when she was struck on her starboard side amidships by the class C-2 freighter, Green Bay. The Captain of the Green Bay, Tom Mazzella, had apparently misinterpreted the location of the *Lightship* on his radar. The Green Bay, which had been navigating through a thick fog at the time, was not seriously damaged, but the *Lightship* went down within ten minutes. All of her crew of nine were rescued without being injured.

In October of 1976, a group of divers, led by Al Catalfumo, made six trips to the site and recovered one of her 60 foot long, 6000 pound light masts. According to Al, the mast can now be viewed in front of a dive shop in Laurence Harbor, N.J.

The *Lightship* now rests upright in 110 feet of water, just east of the Ambrose Tower. She remains relatively intact with the exception of her light masts that were wire dragged down, so as not to cause a hazard to navigation. This three dimensional wreck is excellent for the experienced wreck diver. Visibility is usually good but is also normally dark.

REPUBLIC

The *Republic* was a 570 foot by 67.8 foot White Star Line steamship. She was built in 1903, weighed 15,378 tons and was powered by 1,180 nhp quadruple expansion engines.

The *Republic*. Photo courtesy Steamship Historical Society Collection, University of Baltimore Library.

The *Republic*, after the collision, with a large canvas collision mat strapped to her port side. This attempt to save her failed, she is now sitting in 240 feet of water. Photo courtesy Steamship Historical Society Collection, University of Baltimore Library.

The Italian steamship, Florida, which rammed and sunk the *Republic*, under repair in a New York ship yard. Photo courtesy Suffolk Marine Museum, Sayville, New York.

Due to dense fog on January 23, 1909, the Italian steamship, Florida, rammed the *Republic* on her port side. Two passengers were crushed to death immediately. For the first time in maritime history, a wireless was used to summon aid. The R.C. Gresham and the destroyer, Seneca rushed to the disaster site. All remaining passengers and crew were rescued without mishap. The huge hole in the *Republic's* side was plugged with a make shift collision mat made from canvas. The *Republic* was then taken in tow by the Gresham, but before reaching shallow water, she sank. The *Republic* had remained afloat for 39 hours after her collision.

Aside from being the first to use a wireless, the *Republic* had two other interesting aspects. She was the largest vessel of her day to have sunk, and it is rumored that she was carrying three million dollars in U.S. gold "eagles", worth about one and a half billion dollars today. Apparently, the coins were en route from the U.S. Mint to the Bank of France. Although it's not documented as to which ship was used for transportation, we do know that France never received the coins, hence the conclusion by many marine historians and treasure hunters is that the treasure is still aboard the *Republic*.

In August of 1981, Captain Steve Bielenda of the Research Vessel Wahoo located the *Republic's* resting place. She is leaning slightly to her port side in 240 feet of water, 26 miles south of Nantucket.

In 1987, at least two salvage operations attempted to locate the gold. After extensive research and a costly expedition, both failed. Maybe the gold doesn't really exist, or maybe it's waiting for the right explorer to solve the mystery.

R.P. RESOR

The *R.P. Resor* was built in 1935 by Federal Ship Building Co. in Kearney, New Jersey, she was launched on Saturday, November 13, 1935. She was a 445 foot long, 66 foot wide tanker and was owned by Standard Oil Company (Exxon Corp). The *R.P. Resor* was the first vessel built in the United States on the Isherwood Arcform hull design. The *Resor* was also the first new ship to be fitted with a Contra Guide propeller and rudder, which instead of being symmetrically streamlined is warped. This system claims to add more speed and better maneuverability at the same power. She displaced 7,451 tons and was under the command of Captain Frederick Marcus.

On February 27, 1942, the *R.P. Resor* was traveling from Houston, Texas,

The *R.P. Resor* was built in Kearney New Jersey. She was 445 foot long, 66 foot wide and displaced 7,451 tons. Photo courtesy Steamship Historical Society Collection, University of Baltimore Library.

The U-578 fired two torpedoes into the *Resor*. The second ruptured the tankers oil tanks, setting fire to her. Photo courtesy Bettmann News photos, UPI, New York.

The *Resor* stayed afloat for two days, burning the whole time. Photo courtesy National Archives, Washington, D.C.

to Fall River, Massachusetts, with 78,729 full barrels of crude oil in her holds. Seaman Forsdale was on lookout duty. He spotted a ship off the port bow with its running lights on. Forsdale thought it was a fishing smack and reported his sighting to the bridge. This, however, was just a ruse allowing the German Submarine U-578 (Rehwinkel) to maneuver to within 200 yards before firing a torpedo which exploded amidships. The U-boat then fired another torpedo which ruptured the *Resor's* oil tanks, setting fire to her, and to the oil covered waters around her. As flames enveloped the tanker, men leaped into the water or tried to launch lifeboats. Out of a crew of 41 plus nine naval armed guards, only two survived, one being a crew member and the other a navy guard. The two that survived her initial explosion and fire were almost lost while being rescued. Crude oil from the sinking vessel had covered both men making them heavy and extremely slippery. Chief boatswains mate, John Daise, commander of the Coast Guard picket that rescued both survivors said that the men were coated with thick, congealed oil and weighed over 600 pounds. The Coast Guard cut the men's clothes off to lighten them. Daisy went on to say that even the survivors mouths

Diver with a brass cage lamp found in the stern section of the *Resor* wreck. Photo by Pete Nawrocky.

Tom Roach and Dan Bressette with telegraph from the *Resor*. Photo courtesy Captain George Hoffman.

were filled with a blob of oil. Fortunately, the rescuers were diligent and finally did succeed in lifting the half drowned exhausted men to their safety.

The *Resor* stayed afloat for two more days, burning the whole time. Crowds thronged to the beaches at Asbury Park to watch flames billow up on the horizion. The U.S.S. Sagamore made a futile attempt to tow her ashore for salvage, but the sinking ship's stern bottomed out in 130 feet of water. Soon after, the *Resor* rolled over and slipped beneath the waves. The *Resor* was the 24th ship and 15th tanker sunk or damaged in U.S. coastal waters since the U-Boat campaign had begun.

The *Resor* is now a prominent offshore dive site. Her stern, which is intact, rests on an angle in 130 feet of water. Her stern deck gun, still in place, points to the clean sand bottom. Most of her remains are scattered and low lying. The wreck is known for holding big lobsters and for the amount of brass cage lamps found in her stern section.

While writing this text, I received a letter from Mrs. Judy Baird. Judy's grandfather was Mr. Reuben Perry Resor, treasurer of Standard Oil. Judy went on to tell me that her grandmother had christened the vessel and the family still has the broken champagne bottle used in the christening ceremony which was mounted on a plaque by Standard Oil and presented to Judy's grandmother.

RICKSECKERS

This is the remains of an unidentified vessel which we located in August of 1986. She appears to be an old paddle wheel steamship, but this is only speculation and has yet to be confirmed. The only artifact I've found on this little wreck was a perfume bottle with the name "*Rickseckers* Perfume" on it, hence the name, *Rickseckers*.

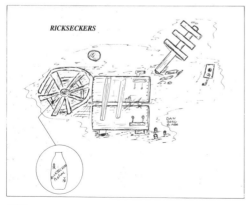

1986 sketch of the *Rickseckers* wreck, also known as the *Engine Wreck*. By Daniel Berg.

She rests on a sandy bottom northeast of Ambrose Light Tower in 66 feet of water. All that remains unburied is her paddle wheel, boilers and some scattered debris. In 1989, while talking with John Lachenmayer and Frank Persico, I found out that this wreck, which I thought we had discovered, is also known as the *Engine Wreck* to the Aquarians dive club which has been frequenting it for years.

ROBERT A. SNOW

The *Robert A. Snow*, which was built in Rockland, Maine, in 1886, is also known to many local divers as the *Derrick Barge*. On February 8, 1899, the schooner, while bound from Barren Island to Rockaway Inlet, sank with her cargo of fertilizer. She now lies two miles northeast of Rockaway Point in 23 feet of water. Her boilers, ribs and some machinery can still be seen. This wreck is excellent for fishing or spearing blackfish.

RODA

Built by A. McMillan & Son, Ltd; Dumbarton in 1897 and owned by the C.T. Bowring & Company, the *Roda* was 315 feet long by 44 feet wide. She displaced 2,516 tons and was powered by a 263 nhp tipple expansion engine.

This old post card shows the *Roda* wreck aground near Today Beach. Photo courtesy Suffolk Marine Museum, Sayville, N.Y.

On February 13, 1908, while on a voyage from Huelva, Spain, to New York, carrying a full cargo of copper ore, the *Roda* was driven aground by an icy eastern gale onto what is today called Tobay Beach. All of the *Roda's* crew were saved in what was called "The most heroic rescue on the Long Island coast in the winter of 1908".

The *Roda* broke in two shortly after running aground, thus spilling her cargo into the sea. She remained visible for a few years until a storm broke her rusted skeleton and finally sent her to the ocean floor.

Today the *Roda* rests in 20 to 30 feet of water, one half mile offshore. Her twisted remains and cargo are spread all over the sea bed. As far as diving this wreck, the surge in this area requires some experience, yet, on a calm day, she is almost within swimming distance from the beach. Fishermen and boaters should be aware that the ships bow and stern stem, plus some ribs, come to within inches of the surface. I have only anchored over this site twice; each time I found that not more than five feet from my boat was wreckage that came within inches of the surface. If you want to dive or fish over this site, I recommend extreme care since many propellers have been bent on the extremities of this wreck.

U.S.S. SAN DIEGO (Armored Cruiser 6)

Originally launched as the *California* on April 28, 1904, by Union Iron Works in San Francisco, she was commissioned on August 1, 1907. She was 503'11" long by 69'77" wide and had a displacement of 13,680 tons. She served as part of Theodore Roosevelt's Great White Fleet. Her twin props pushed her at a top speed of 22 knots. The warship's armament consisted of 18 three inch guns, 14 six inch guns mounted in side turrets, four eight inch guns and two 18 inch torpedo tubes. On September 1, 1914, she was renamed *San Diego* and served as the flag ship for our Pacific fleet. On July 18, 1917, she was ordered to the Atlantic to escort convoys through the first dangerous leg of their journey to Europe. The *Diego* held a perfect record, safely escorting all the ships she was assigned through the submarine infested North Atlantic without mishaps.

On July 8, 1918, the *San Diego* left Portsmouth, New Hampshire, en route to New York. She had rounded Nantucket Light and was heading west. On July 19, 1918, she was zig-zagging as per war instructions on course to New York. Sea was smooth, the visibility 6 miles. At 11:23 AM, an ear shattering explosion tore a huge hole in her port side amidships. Captain Christy immediately sounded submarine defense quarters, which involves a general alarm and the closing of all water-tight doors. Soon after, two more

U.S.S. California under steam. Photo courtesy National Archives.

On September 1, 1914 the *California* was recommissioned *San Diego*. Photo courtesy National Archives.

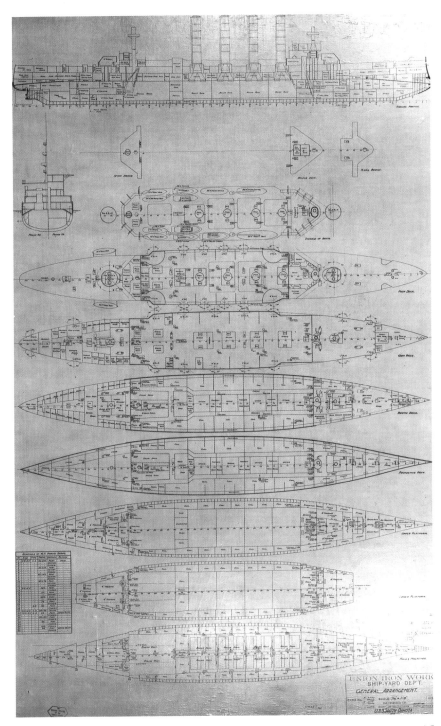

UNION IRON WORKS
SHIP-YARD DEPT.
GENERAL ARRANGEMENT.

U.S.S. SOUTH DAKOTA

125

explosions ripped through her hull. These secondary explosions were determined later to be caused by the rupturing of one of her boilers and ignition of her magazine. The ship immediately started to list to port. Officers and crew quickly went to their stations. Guns were fired from all sides of the war ship at anything that was taken for a possible periscope. Her port guns fired until they were awash. Her starboard guns fired until the list of the ship pointed them into the sky. Under the impression that a submarine was surely in the area, the men stayed at their posts until Captain Christy shouted the order "All hands abandon ship". In a last ditch effort to save his ship, Captain H. Christy had steamed toward Fire Island Beach, but never made it. At 11:51 AM the *Diego* sank, only 28 minutes after the initial explosion. In accordance with navy tradition, Captain Christy was the last man to leave his ship. As the vessel was turning over, he made his way from the bridge down two ladders to the boat deck over the side to the armor belt, dropped four feet to the bilge keel and finally jumped overboard from the docking keel which was then only eight feet from the water. As the Captain left his ship, men in the life boats cheered him and started to sing our National Anthem. Most survivors were picked up by nearby vessels, but at least four life boats full of men rowed ashore, three at Bellport and one near the Lone Hill Coast Guard Station. The *San Diego* was the only major warship lost by the United States in World War I.

The original casualty reports ranged from 30 to 40. Apparently, the muster roll on the *San Diego* was not saved. The only list of men on board was the

Painting of the *U.S.S. San Diego* sinking. Courtesy National Archives.

Underwater photograph of the *Diego's* propeller, which has since been removed. Photo by Mike DeCamp.

payroll of June 30, but since the end of June, they had received and transferred over 100 men. When the Navy eventually finalized the death toll, the official count was only six.

Since her sinking, there has been much debate about whether it was a torpedo, German mine or U.S. mine that sent the cruiser to Davy Jones Locker. Captain Christy wrote in his final log that they had been hit by a torpedo. The Navy, however, found and destroyed five or six German surface mines in the vicinity, so it is generally accepted that a mine laid by the U-156 did the job. Ironically, the U-156 was sunk on its homeward journey possibly by a U.S. mine.

On July 26, 1918, the U.S.S. Passaio arrived over the wreck. Two divers were sent down to report on the condition of the *San Diego*. They reported the following; "Many loose rivets lying on the bottom. ... Masts and smoke stack are lying on the bottom under and on starboard side of ship. ... Ship lies heading about North depth of water over starboard bilge is 36 feet. ... Air is still coming out of the ship from nearly bow to stern. It seems likely that as air escapes and she loses buoyancy, she may crush her superstructure and settle deeper". From this report the Navy concluded that the vessel was not salvageable. As quoted from their letter to the Chief of Naval Operations," In view of the reported condition and position of the *San Diego*, the Bureau is of the opinion that an attempt to salvage the vessel as a whole, or to recover any of the guns, would not be warranted". They did, however, have concerns about the site being a hazard to navigation and the possibility of dynamiting her to increase the available depth of water over the wreck. On October 15, the U.S.S. Resolute took another sounding on the site. It found that the wreck had settled slightly and now had 40 feet of water over her, so the wreck was not blown up.

In 1962, salvage rights to the *San Diego* were sold for $14,000: The salvage company planned to blow up the wreck for scrap metal. Several groups including the American Littoral Society, Marine Angling Club and National Party Boat Owners Association banded together and lobbied. After a lot of bad publicity, public outcry and a financial compensation, the salvage company agreed to give up the job. The wreck, now an artificial reef, supports teeming amounts of aquatic life, not to mention many charter boat operations.

Another interesting side step to the *Diego* story occurred when a Long Island diver attempted to raise the one remaining, 18 foot in diameter, 37,000 pound bronze prop. He succeeded only in sinking his barge mounted crane which now rests on the bottom a short distance from the *Diego's* stern. This barge has herself become a good lobstering dive. Someone else made off with the valued prop.

Barge mounted crane which was used in an attempt to salvage the *Diego* wrecks propeller. Photo courtesy Ed Betts.

Propeller salvage operation succeeded only in sinking of the crane barge. The Barge now rests a short distance from the *Diego's* stern. Photo courtesy Ed Betts.

The *San Diego's* propeller was latter raised by another outfit. Photo courtesy Steve Bielenda.

Diego's propeller being lifted onto a barge. Photo courtesy Steve Bielenda.

129

Underwater sketch of the *San Diego*. Courtesy Gary Gentile and Kathy Warehouse.

On June 3, 1982, the N.Y. POST reported that the bomb squad had been tipped off that a local diver had recovered a two foot long, five inch diameter artillery shell from the *San Diego*. The diver had planned to sand blast it and stand it next to his fire place. The shell was confiscated, but because it was too powerful for Suffolk's detonation site it had to be transported to Ft. Dix, New Jersey and detonated by the Army. Lt. Thomas, commander of the Suffolk bomb squad, said, "it's the biggest warhead I've ever seen; it could go off just from drying out".

Ammunition Room. Photo by Pete Nawrocky.

Stack of gun powder canisters. Photo by Steve Bielenda.

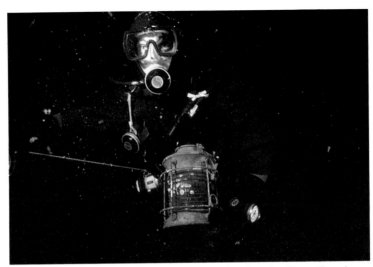

A diver starts his ascent with a beautiful lantern found on the *Diego*. Photo by Pete Nawrocky.

Lantern from *San Diego* wreck. Photo by Pete Nawrocky.

A diver exits the china room with a bowl. Photo by Pete Nawrocky.

131

The author, Dan Berg, holds
the storm door of an exterior
hatch mounted porthole open.
Photo by Steve Bielenda.

Five pound lobster on the
San Diego. Photo by
Daniel Berg.

China from the *San Diego*.

Frank Persico holds four lanterns he found on the *Diego*.

Diver Bill Campbell and Dan Berg with a brass door frame. Photo by Steve Bielenda.

Sally Wahrmann and Hank Garvin with officers china and a silver platter. Photo by Steve Bielenda.

Helm recovered and photographed by Captain John Lachenmayer.

This brass explosion proof light was found by Bill Campbell while exploring a newly opened area on the *San Diego* wreck. Photo by Dan Derg.

Porthole swing plate recovered by the author. Photo by Steve Bielenda.

Brass Lantern. Photo by George Quirk.

Brass Lantern from the *San Diego*. Photo by Pete Nawrocky.

Brass Razor found inside the *San Diego* wreck. Photo by Pete Nawrocky.

135

San Diego

On October 8, 1987, the research vessel Wahoo, captained by Steve Bielenda, ran a special trip to the *San Diego*. Aboard were some of the east coast's top wreck divers like Hank Keats, author of DIVE INTO HISTORY, Captain John Lachenmayer, Hank Garvin, Janet Bieser and myself. All participated in a dive to photograph, video and recover artifacts from a newly discovered storage room that George Quirk had located in the bow of this WW I cruiser. John Lachenmeyer entered the water and secured the anchor line to the wreck. He was soon followed by Hank and I who swam forward, then dropped down the starboard side to the location of a small corroded hole in the outer hull. We penetrated to the interior of the wreck. Hank reached a small room and took some photographs. As he backed off I proceeded to video an intact supply room, full of china dishes, bowls and silverware. This was to be the only view of the china room that day. Divers pulling artifacts from the silt covered floor reduced visibility to zero. As fresh teams of divers swam down to the wreck, lift bags popped to the surface carrying mesh bags filled with china, silverware and even lanterns. Many of the artifacts recovered on this very successful day were donated to local museums, used to decorate area dive shops or are incorporated into slide shows, TV shows and magazine articles, all aimed at increasing the public's interest in diving and shipwrecks.

Today, the *Diego* lies upside down and relatively intact in 110 feet of water, 13.5 miles out of Fire Island Inlet. One of the nicest aspects of this wreck is that it can be enjoyed at various depths. Divers can reach her hull in approximately 65 feet of water while her stern ammo room is in 90 feet and her stern wash out reaches a maximum depth of 116 feet of water. Besides supporting a huge array of fish life, she is one of Long Island's scuba diving hot spots. Divers can find artifacts such as bullets, portholes, cage lamps, china and brass valves. The portholes found on this wreck are unique. They are made up of three parts, each of which is serial numbered: the backing plate, which is bolted into her armor plating, a swing plate window and a brass storm cover. What makes these portholes desirable to sport divers is the fact that the backing plates are almost impossible to unbolt while underwater. This means that while many divers have swing plates or storm covers, very few have a complete set and even fewer have a set with matching serial numbers.

Two years ago, Steve Bielenda and I were diving on the *Diego*. I swam inside a gun turret where I caught a five pound lobster. When I turned around, I found a brass cage lamp and when I exited the wreck, there sitting half buried in the sand below me was an intact porthole. That was definitely one of my more productive dives. My next porthole from this wreck was not as easy and required approximately 15 working dives to recover. For the underwater photographer, this wreck provides structures, hallways and compartments which all make for beautiful photos.

136

SANDY HOOK

The *Sandy Hook* was built at the Crescent Ship Yard in Elizabeth, New Jersey, back in 1902. She was originally named the *Anstice* when sailing as a private steam yacht. She was later renamed the *Privateer* and finally *Sandy Hook* when commissioned and refitted as a pilot boat in 1914.

On April 27, 1939, while sailing in a dense fog, the steam powered, 361 ton pilot boat was rammed aft of the port beam and sunk by the Norwegian ship, Oslofjord. All 20 pilots and six crew members were rescued with little or no injuries. Robert Peterson, one of the pilots aboard the *Sandy Hook*, gave the following account to the NEW YORK POST. "I was in the main saloon, prepared to board the vessel as she neared. Suddenly I looked out the porthole and there was the bow of the boat almost on top of us. I jumped and ran out of the cabin. The next instant, she hit us. Everybody ran for the boats as mast and booms crashed on deck smashing a life boat".

The *Privateer* would later be converted into a pilot boat and re-named *Sandy Hook*. Photo courtesy Frank Litter.

Privateer in dry dock while being converted into a pilot boat. Photo courtesy Frank Persico collection.

Pilot boat *Sandy Hook*. Photo courtesy Captain Frank Persico collection.

This small green glass pitcher was found by Rick Schwarz. Photo by Daniel Berg.

Ornate wall lamp, found and photographed by Frank Persico.

Porthole the author raised from the *Sandy Hook*. Photo by Dennis Berg

**PILOT BOAT
SUNK 4/27/39**

Today, the *Sandy Hook* rests in 100 feet of water just east of Ambrose Tower. Sketch by Daniel Berg.

A side story to the *Sandy Hook's* sinking is the presence of royalty aboard the Oslofjord. Crown Prince Olav and Princess Martha of Norway, on their way to visit President Roosevelt, were slightly detained due to the accident. The Prince reported that on board the Oslofjord they barely even felt the collision that sent one vessel to the bottom.

About four years ago, I ran my boat to this wreck. Diving partners Rick Schwarz, Dennis Berg and I descended and within ten minutes, I had sent a porthole to the surface. Unfortunately it was still attached to a steel hull plate and required a 500 pound lift bag. Although we tried, we couldn't get the cumbersome artifact onto the boat, and had to cut it free. We have made many dives on this wreck since then, but I've never been able to relocate the porthole. I figure, it's lying in the sand somewhere, just east of her bow section.

Today, the *Sandy Hook*, also known as the *Pilot Boat* wreck, rests in 100 feet of water just east of Ambrose Light Tower, seven miles southwest of Debs Inlet. Her bow is broken and lies on its starboard side. Behind the bow lies a debris field, and further back sits the intact stern section. The water over this wreck is usually clear but also dark. Everything from portholes to lamps and glassware has been recovered from this site.

The 340 foot long *Sommerstad*. Photo courtesy Peabody Museum, Salem, Mass.

SOMMERSTAD

Many years ago captain Jay Porter announced to his crew that he had found a virgin wreck. One of the paying customers on his boat over heard him, but thought he said "*Virginia*", hence the wreck's given name.

Just recently, ship historian Eric Gary concluded through much research that the wreck we know as *Virginia* is really a ship called *Sommerstad*. Although no artifacts that have been brought up off of the wreck positively identify her, all evidence backs up Eric's research.

The *Sommerstad* was built in 1906 in Newcastle, England. She was 340 feet long by 47 feet wide and displaced 3,875 tons. She was powered by 301 nhp triple expansion engines and was owned by A.F. Klaveness Company.

On August 12, 1918, while bound from Norway to New York under the command of Captain George Hansen, the *Sommerstad* was sunk by the German submarine U-117. The U-117 had fired a torpedo at her starboard side. The lookout man on board *Sommerstad* reported sighting the wake from the torpedo and watched as it just missed his ship's bow. The torpedo then did something very strange and horrifying; it turned around and headed back, striking the *Sommerstad* amidships on her port side. Within minutes, she was gone. Later some would speculate that the German torpedo was radio controlled, but U.S. Naval experts were convinced that the torpedos gyroscope was not working correctly, causing the abnormal

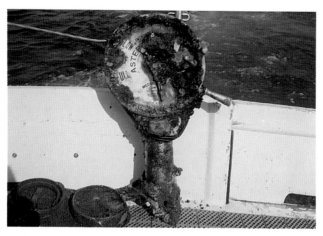

Telegraph recovered from the *Virginia*. Photo by John Lachenmayer.

path. The entire crew had the good fortune of escaping with just a few minor injuries. All 31 men rowed for a full day before being spotted by the Coast Guard.

The *Sommerstad* or *Virginia*, as she is more commonly known, rests in 180 feet of water 36 miles from Fire Island Inlet. Captain John Lachenmayer describes her as looking like the *Iberia* wreck but larger, with her propeller and boilers easily recognizable.

SPARTAN

The *Spartan* was an 85 foot by 24 foot canal tugboat. She was built in Chicago in 1957 and was sunk as a fish haven on January 31, 1986.

The tugboat *Spartan* sinks stern first into 70 feet of water. Photo courtesy Bill Figely.

According to Herb Segars, a noted underwater photographer, her remains are sitting perfectly upright in 70 feet of water, three miles off Manasquan Inlet. Herb goes on to say that mussels and anemones are abundant and the visibility is usually excellent.

STEAMSHIP

The *Steamship* wreck rests in 60 to 70 feet of water two miles west of Ambrose Light Tower. Although she is a big wreck with lots of brass artifacts on her, no one, to the best of my knowledge, has been able to positively identify her. Bill Reddan, a local charter captain, refers to this wreck as *Martins Misery*; the wreck is known to others as the *Eastern Steamship*.

STEEL WRECK

The name of this wreck may be forever a mystery. She was a square masted wooden vessel carrying a cargo of wire products and bed springs when she sunk. The *Steel Wreck*, or as she is also known, the *Wire Wreck*, rests five miles out of Jones Inlet in 75 feet of water. Her hull is broken up with only two sections of her ribs remaining. All around her are the piles of wire and rusted steel that she was carrying, which now provide a good home for lobsters and other crustaceans. John Lachenmayer tells me that portholes from this wreck are octagonal in shape and make a very unique artifact.

STOLT DAGALI

The *Stolt Dagali* was a 583 foot, 19,150 ton Norwegian steel hulled tanker. She was built in 1955 in Denmark by Burmeister & Wain shipbuilders.

On November 26, 1964 (Thanksgiving Day), while carrying a cargo of vegetable and coconut oil from Philadelphia to Newark, she entered a dense fog bank. Within minutes of entering the fog, the bow of the 629 foot Israeli luxury liner, S.S. Shalom, which was outbound for a Caribbean cruise, collided with the *Stolt Dagali's* port side, sheering off her stern. A total of 19 crew members lost their lives in the nearly 50 degree water. Most of the men killed were sleeping in the 140 foot stern section which sank in minutes. The lucky men who were on the bow of the vessel including Captain Kristian Bendiksen and nine others were rescued by various Coast Guard crafts which consisted of seven Cutters and at least five helicopters from Floyd Bennett station.

143

Stolt Dagali

The 593 foot Norwegian tanker *Stolt Dagali,* Photo courtesy Marine Publications International.

The SS Shalom was not fatally wounded but did suffer a 40 foot gash on her starboard side as a result of the collision. The Shalom and the *Stolt Dagali's* bow section, which stayed afloat, were towed to the port of New York by two Moran tugs escorted by Coast Guard Cutters. The *Stolt's* bow was eventually partially salvaged.

The *Stolt Dagali's* bow was towed to the port of New York. Photo courtesy U.S. Coast Guard.

Chuck Zimmaro sketched the *Stolt's* stern as she sits today in 130 feet of water. © Charles P. Zimmaro 1990.

Diver exploring the *Stolt's* stern section. Photo by Jozef Koppelman.

Stolt Dagali underwater. Photo courtesy Jozef Koppelman.

Deep inside the *Stolt's* stern, a diver searches for artifacts. Photo courtesy Jozef Koppelman.

Exiting the wreck.
Photo by Jozef Koppelman.

Stolt Dagali

Helm from the *Stolt Dagali*. Courtesy George Hoffman.

Underwater photo of the *Stolt Dagali's* engine telegraph. Courtesy George Hoffman.

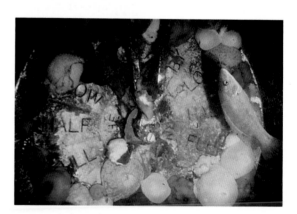

China, silverware, and lobsters from the *Stolt Dagali*. Photo courtesy George Hoffman.

Today, a 140 foot piece of the *Stolt Dagali's* stern rests on its starboard side 36 miles out of Debs Inlet and 18 miles from Manasquan Inlet. Her remains lie in 130 feet of water, but rise to within 65 feet of the surface, providing an artificial reef for all types of aquatic life and a hot spot for divers and fishermen alike.

STONE BARGE

The *Stone Barge* lies three miles southeast of Jones Inlet. She sunk while carrying a cargo of cut granite jetty rocks, supposedly to be used for the Jones Beach jetty. As the story goes, the tug *Edwin Duke* that was towing the barge also went down in the same storm and now rests a short distance away.

Today, most of the barge has either been buried or deteriorated although some wood still remains on the north east side. The long pile of stones remaining above sand lies in 55 feet of water and makes a good habitat for lobsters and fish. Her location, so close to the inlet, makes her a very popular spot especially on summer weekends. It isn't uncommon to have five or ten boats anchored over the wreck at any one time.

SUFFOLK

The *Suffolk* was a coal coiler, built in 1911 by New York Ship Building, Camden, New Jersey. She was owned by Sprag Steamship Co. located in Boston. She was 366 feet long, had a 50 foot beam and displaced 4,607 gross tons.

Rare photograph of the coal coiler *Suffolk*. Courtesy Frank Persico collection.

Suffolk

On December 11, 1943, while en route from Norfolk to Boston with a cargo of coal, she was caught in a northeast gale. The steel hulled coiler couldn't take the pounding and went down, taking all 36 crew and six Navy armed guards with her.

Don Schnell (left) and Mark Hill hold two huge lobsters from the *Suffolk* wreck. Photo courtesy Steve Bielenda.

According to Captain Steve Bielenda, the *Suffolk* is now sitting in 180 to 190 feet of water approximately 25 miles south of Montauk Point. She is broken in two with her stern resting at a right angle to her main wreckage. The stern is resting on her side while the rest of the vessel is upside down. This wreck is heavily fished for cod and pollack and is literally covered with high test monofilament. Hank Garvin, who is one of only a hand full of divers to visit this wreck, confirms reports of heavy monofilament on the wreck and went on to tell me of a diver who was so entangled in the fishing line that if it weren't for his buddy, he would not have been able to cut his way out. To say the least, this wreck is only for the experienced deep diver and is definitely a two knife dive.

U.S.S. TARANTULA

Commonly known as the *Gun Boat*, the identity of this wreck had been unknown since she was originally located by Jay Porter. She was given the name *Gun Boat* by divers who noticed the armament that she had carried.

In 1985, Billy "Bubbles" deMarigny, a local diver, found and recovered the ship's brass bell. Inscribed on the bell was the ship's true name, *Tarantula*.

The private steam yacht *Tarantula*. Photo courtesy SPNEA, Boston.

Tarantula

The *Tarantula* after being converted into a gun boat. Courtesy Bill deMarigny.

In 1985 Billy deMarigny found and recovered the ships brass bell. Photo by Daniel Berg.

The *Tarantula* was a private steam yacht. But why would a yacht be armored?. Through some research, I believe I've found the answer.

While researching the name, *Tarantula*, I came across two ships. Both were yachts owned by W.K. Vanderbilt, one built in 1902 and the other in 1912. I thought I had found the answer when I read that the ship built in 1902 had been commissioned by the Canadian Navy during WWI. This ship was renamed the H.M.C.S. Tuna and would have certainly explained the wreck's guns, but unfortunately my early assumption was wrong. The Tuna had never sunk; she was sold in 1918 and eventually stripped for salvage. The *Gun Boat* wreck off of Long Island was the 128 foot by 19 foot, 159 ton *U.S.S. Tarantula*, built by George Lawley and Son Corp in 1912. She was in service with the U.S.Navy at the time of her loss. After a collision with the Royal Holland Loyd Line steamship, SS Frisia, on October 28, 1918, the *Tarantula* sunk.

Angler fish on the *Tarantula*.
Photo by Pete Nawrocky.

Ammunition can still be found on the *Tarantula*
wreck. Photo's by Peter Nawrocky.

China and silverware
recovered from the *Tarantula*.
Photo By Pete Nawrocky.

153

Fluted anchor raised by Steve Jonassen (left) and Dan Berg. Photo by Bill Campbell.

In 1988, Steve Bielenda and I were filming the marine life on this wreck. I was filming a three foot Angler fish swimming over some low lying wreckage when we both noticed the outline of another angler fish hidden in the sand. The second fish was huge, almost five feet long and most definitely the largest fish of this species either Steve or I have ever seen. We also found a few 40 pound cod fish and an eight pound lobster. We were both amazed at the quantity and size of the marine life inhabiting this little wreck.

Today, the *U.S.S. Tarantula* lies 22 miles off Jones Inlet in 115 feet of water. If you want to dive on her or fish over this wreck, most captains know her as the *Good Gun Boat* wreck. The remains are very low lying with only her boilers coming off the bottom about seven feet. She lies in a straight line. Her bow, which only protrudes about three feet off the bottom, still has a navy anchor in place on the starboard side. Divers can dig just ahead of the boilers for ammunition or behind the boilers for china and silverware.

TEXAS TOWER

The *Texas Tower No. 4* was a triangular shaped Air Force Radar Tower, or

U.S. Air Force *Texas Tower No. 4.* Photo courtesy U.S. Air Force.

Today the *Tower* rests in 180 feet of water, her wreckage rise to within 70 feet of the surface. Sketch © Charles P. Zimmaro 1990.

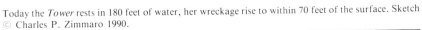

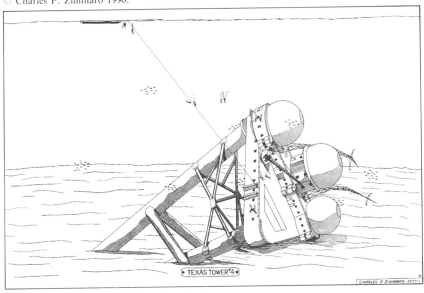

155

Texts Tower

Texas Tower. Photo by Jozef Koppelman.

Window on the *Texas Tower* wreck. Photo by Pete Nawrocky.

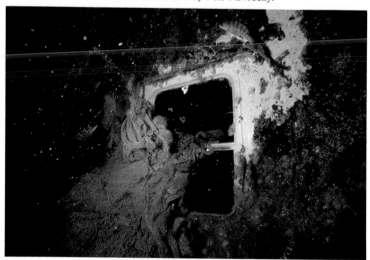

D.E.W. (Distant Early Warning) built in Portland, Maine, back in 1957. The three deck platform weighed 500 tons and stood 67 feet above sea level.

On August 29, 1958, Daisy, the first of two hurricanes, severely damaged the radar station. Hurricane Donna hit in September of 1960, inflicting even more damage to the *Tower's* already weakened underwater legs. By this time, the crew had nicknamed the tower, *Old Shaky.* In November, 1960, all but 14 crew and 14 repairmen were evacuated for safety reasons. By early January, conditions on board had worsened, but the Air Force would not evacuate for fear that nearby Russian trawlers would capture the abandoned tower and the electronics within her. By the second week of January with 50 knot winds and 30 foot seas enveloping the tower, the crew on *Old Shaky* feared for their lives. Evacuation orders were finally received and the aircraft carrier, Wasp, rushed to the rescue. At 6:00 PM the tower radioed "the tower is breaking up". At 7:20 PM Captain Mangual in a rescue craft had his eyes fastened on the towers radar image "suddenly the image blurs and is gone" Mangual tried to radio *Tower No. 4.* There was no reply. It was too late. At 7:33 PM, Sunday January 15, 1961, the *Texas Tower* slid into the ocean, taking all 28 men to their deaths.

After the tragedy, only one body was recovered. Hopes were raised when the Navy picked up knocking sounds on its sonar. The opinion was that some men could still be alive, trapped in an air space. Unfortunately, none of the men were ever found.

Today the *Tower* rests in 180 feet of water 58 miles out of Fire Island Inlet. Although this huge structure really doesn't classify as a ship wreck, her broken bones which rise to within 70 feet of the surface host an incredible amount and variety of marine life.

THREE SISTERS

Sketch of the *Three Sisters* wreck. By Dan Berg.

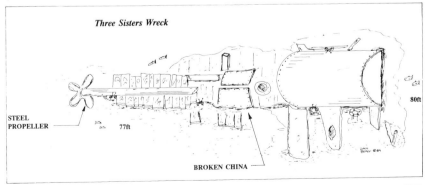

The *Three Sisters* is yet another of *Wreck Valley's* unidentified ship wrecks. Her scattered wooden remains sit in 75 to 80 feet of water 13 miles south of Atlantic Beach Inlet. All that remains to be seen on this wreck is her boiler, some low lying wood wreckage and a large four bladed steel propeller. Judging from the size of her propeller and boiler, this vessel could have been about 80 feet long and possibly the remains of a tug boat. George Quirk found a brass valve that was dated to the early 1800's on her. Whatever she was, this little wreck produces considerable amounts of fish and lobsters, but due to her size is best for small groups of divers.

TOLTEN

Formerly named the *S.S. Lotta*, the *Tolten*, a 280 foot by 43 foot Danish steamer, was taken over and renamed by the Chilean government when WW II began in Europe. She was built in 1938, displaced 1,858 gross tons and had the distinct misfortune of being the first Chilean vessel sunk during the war.

The *S.S. Lotta* would latter become the *Tolten*. Photo courtesy Dan Berg collection.

On March 13, 1942, the *Tolten*, having unloaded her cargo of nitrates a day earlier, was travelling in ballast to New York when she was struck by a pair of German torpedoes fired from the U-404. The subsequent explosions ripped the ship apart, sending her to the bottom within six minutes. At the time of her sinking, Chile was a neutral country and had been assured by Germany that none of her ships would be attacked as long as they travelled with their running lights on. The *Tolten* had been stopped before her attack by a U.S. Navy patrol boat and had been warned to be on the lookout for submarines and to travel "Blacked Out". Much to her demise, the *Tolten* took the patrol boat's advice. Out of 28 crew members, only the electrician, Julio Faust, survived to tell the story. Julio managed to cling to a life raft for nearly twelve hours before being picked up by a Coast Guard vessel.

Today, The *Tolten's* broken up hull can be found lying on her starboard side in 90 feet of water, 40 miles out of Debs Inlet and 16 miles from Barnegat Inlet. Since her sinking, she has been wire dragged clear to a depth of 50 feet, so as not to be a hazard to navigation.

U.S.S. TURNER

The *U.S.S. Turner* was a Bristol class destroyer built in Kearny, New Jersey, in November, 1942. Commissioned on April 15, 1943, she was 350 feet by 36 feet and weighed 1,700 tons. Her armament consisted of 4 five inch guns, 10 torpedo tubes and both 20 mm and 40 mm anti-aircraft guns.

On January 3, 1944, at 6:18 AM, while sitting at anchor about four miles off shore, an explosion tore a tremendous hole in her port side up near the bow. At the same time, the explosion's force brought down the ship's mast destroying all communications and killing all or most of her officers. The NEW YORK TIMES reports "The engine room filled with smoke, but the men stayed at their stations, groping about, some choking, their eyes bloodshot. They kept up enough pressure to work the ship's fire hose".

Back on shore at the Coast Guard station in Sandy Hook, New Jersey, Coxswain F. Williams happened to witness the destroyer's explosion. He set off the general quarters' alarm and within minutes an 83 foot sub chaser, a 77 foot CGR Boat and a pilot boat were all on their way for the rescue mission. When the rescuers arrived, they all worked heroically under exploding artillery shells which were set off by fires on the *Turner*. Soon after, all survivors, totalling 163 men, were removed. The *Turner* exploded a second time. This explosion was so tremendous that its concussion broke house windows up and down the New Jersey and Long Island coasts. Moments later, with a sudden hissing sound, the *Turner* sank beneath the surface.

Although the death toll was never announced because of war time restrictions, there must have been about 30 to 40 lives lost. The *Turners* official cause of sinking was listed as "Due to defective ammunitions," but it is believed she was most likely torpedoed by a German submarine.

The Bristol class destroyer *U.S.S. Turner*. Photo courtesy National Archives.

Compass recovered from the *Turner* wreck by Bill deMarigny. Photo by Dan Berg.

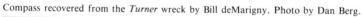

A few years back, an oil tanker scraped her belly on the *Turner* wreck. The resulting oil spill and headlines prompted the Government to partially salvage the *Turner* and to reduce the amount of wreckage. After this action was taken, the *Turner* was no longer a hazard to navigation.

Today, the *Turner* lies in several piles of debris, leaving no recognizable shapes. She rests five miles out of Debs Inlet in 50 to 58 feet of water and proves to be a good in shore wreck for both fishing and diving. Bill Campbell and I have made many dives to the *Turner*. Most were at night in search of lobsters, but on one daylight dive, we decided to dig in the sand on the western edge of her wreckage. Surprisingly, we recovered some old blob top bottles. They were too old to be from the *Turner*, and we have not yet been back for further investigation.

U-853 (German Submarine)

The *U-853*, which had been nick named by her crew "*Der Seiltaenzer*" *Tightrope Walker*, was a type IXC German U-Boat. Commissioned on June 25, 1943, she was 251.9 feet long, 22.5 feet wide and displaced 740 tons.

Rare photograph of the *U-853*. Photo Courtesy Fred Benson.

U-853 which had been nick named *Tightrope Walker*, was a type IXC German submarine. Photo courtesy Fred Benson.

U-853's crew and officers. Photo courtesy Frank Persico collection.

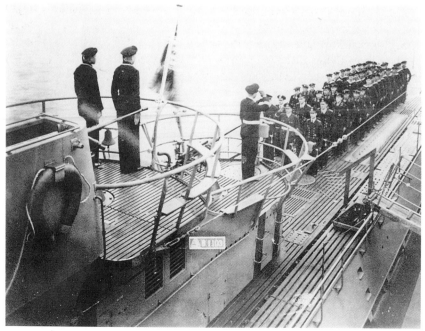

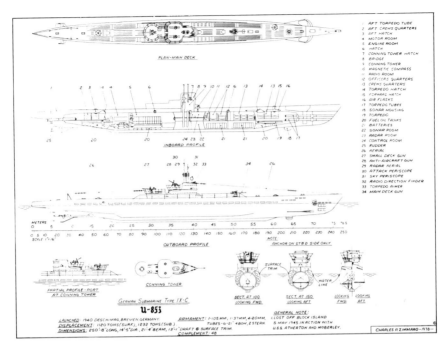

© Charles P. Zimmaro 1990.

On May 1, 1945, Hamburg radio announced that Adolf Hitler was dead. Grand Admiral Doenitz took over as Der Fuehrer and immediately began to arrange a surrender. On May 4, 1945, with WW II quickly coming to an end, Admiral Karl Doenitz gave the following order "All U-boats cease fire at once. Stop all hostile action against allied shipping. Doenitz". We are not sure if the *U-853* received Doenitz's transmission or simply refused to obey his orders. U.S. naval experts at the time considered U-boat captains to be among the most fanatical members of the German military and predicted that some would continue to fight despite Doenitz's order.

On May 5, the *U-853*, which had been prowling the waters northeast of Block Island, torpedoed and sank the coiler *Black Point*, killing twelve men. Two minutes later, the SS Kamen, a Yugoslav freighter, radioed word of the sinking. Within an hour, the U.S. Navy Task force, which was in the area, began hunting the *853*. The Atherton found her within three hours and the attack began. The Navy used Hedgehogs (rocket launched projectiles), depth charges, three ships and two blimps. After an assault with depth charges, various bits of debris floated to the surface including a pillow, a life jacket and the U-boat's captain's hat. This was only a trick as the Navy's sonar then caught the sub moving east. Again and again, resulting in a cat and mouse type game to the death, the Navy's sonar would

163

After an assault with depth charges, various bits of debris floated to the surface, but this was only a trick. Photo courtesy Steve Bielenda collection.

Conning tower of the *U-853*. Courtesy Steve Bielenda.

Diver explores the U-boat wreck. Photo by Jozef Koppelman.

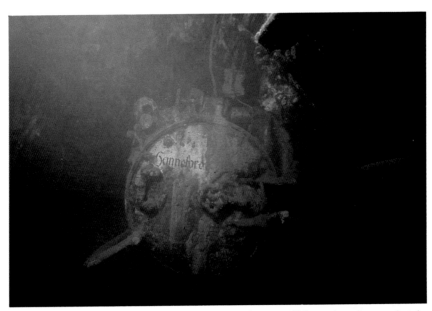

Inside the U-boats forward torpedo room German writing can still be read on the torpedo tube door. Photo by Bill Campbell.

Hatch on the *U-853*. Photo courtesy Bill Campbell.

Gary Gilligan recovered this hatch from the *U-853*. Photo by Steve Bielenda.

locate the U-boat and the attacks would resume. The first attack started at 8:29 PM. The Navy continued its assault until 10:45 AM the next day. The *U-853* was declared officially dead. The Navy vessels headed for port with brooms at masthead, the Navy's symbol for a clean sweep.

On May 6, 1945, Navy divers from the vessel Penguin dove on the *U-853* and attempted to penetrate the wreck in order to recover records from the captain's safe. These divers were using surface supplied air and couldn't easily fit through the tight hatches of the submarine. The next day, Ed Bockelman, the smallest diver on the Penguin, volunteered himself for the task. He was accompanied by Commander George Albin. Bockelman was able to squeeze through the conning towers hatch, but the floating lifeless bodies of German crewmen blocked further penetration.

For years after her sinking, rumors spread that the *U-853* had a cargo of treasure on board. One story claimed that $500,000 in jewels and U.S. currency were hidden in 88 MM shell cases. sealed in wax. Another rumor was that there was $1,000,000 in hidden mercury on board, sealed in stainless steel flasks. These rumors have spurred many salvage attempts over the years, none of which, to the best of my knowledge, have been successful. Who knows, maybe a sport diver will get lucky.

Today, the *U-853* sits in 130 feet of water off Block Island. She is sitting upright and intact on a sand bottom. Penetration of the wreck is possible but should only be a attempted by experienced wreck divers.

VARANGER

Also known under the name 28 *Mile Wreck*, the *Varanger*, was a 9,305 ton Norwegian Tanker. She was built in Amsterdam in 1925 and was owned by Westfal, Larsen & Company.

On January 25, 1942, under the command of Captain Karl Horne, while bound from Curacao to New York, carrying a cargo of 12,750 tons of fuel oil picked up in the West Indies, the ship was struck amidships on her port side by a German torpedo fired from the U-130. The first explosion knocked out the radio room, making it impossible to send a May Day. Within 15 minutes, two more torpedoes struck the *Varanger*, ripping her into three sections and sending her to the bottom. It is still unbelievable that the entire crew was able to escape on two life boats without a single fatality. All were picked up by a fishing boat a few miles away.

The *Varanger*, which was the sixth vessel sunk in U.S. waters by U-boats,

The Norwegian tanker *Varanger*, also known as *28 Mile Wreck*.

Gun mounted on the *Varanger's* deck. Photo courtesy Steamship Historical Society Collection, University of Baltimore Library.

The *Varanger* is sitting upright and relatively intact considering the number of explosions that sank her. Sketch © Charles P. Zimmaro 1990.

rests in 145 feet of water along the 29 fathom curve. The wreck is sitting upright in good condition considering the number of explosions that sank her. In season, the water around her abounds with giant bluefish, cod, bonito, skipjack, shark and on occasion, even marlin have been seen. As mentioned earlier this wreck has been nicknamed *28 Mile Wreck* due to her approximate distance from Brigantine, Great Egg and Absecon Inlets.

WOLCOTT

The *Wolcott* is an unknown schooner. This wreck was found and named by charter boat captain, Jay Porter on the day that Jersey Joe Wolcott beat Joe Louis in boxing's title match.

The *Wolcott* lies very close to the Patchogue fishing grounds, four miles northeast of the *San Diego* wreck in 70 to 80 feet of water. She is a big wreck, very broken up and scattered over a large area. According to Steve Bielenda a huge fluted anchor still can be seen amongst the wreckage. This area is excellent for cod, sea bass and especially lobster.

YANKEE

The *Yankee* was a 296 foot by 40 foot steel hulled coastwise steamer. She was built by Globe Iron Works in December, 1890, and originally named *German*. The *Yankee* displaced 2,418 Gross Tons and was powered by coal fired steam.

On the night of June 11, 1919, while en route from Norfolk, Virginia to Boston, Massachusetts, carrying a cargo of coal, the *Yankee* entered a dense fog. Soon after she collided with the Italian liner, Argentina. The following information is excerpted from the accident report filed with the Secretary of Commerce: "A dense fog prevailed and the vessel was proceeding at a slow speed. ... Suddenly, the lights of the Argentina were seen about two points on the port bow. ... Engines of the *Yankee* were at once stopped but as it was seen that a collision was inevitable, the helm of the *Yankee* was brought hard-a-port". This was done in an effort of paralleling the other vessel and was almost accomplished, but the ships closed in, and the starboard bow of the Argentina struck then sheared off the *Yankee*. This forced the Argentina's stern into the *Yankee's* hull. The Argentina's propeller ripped through, causing a fatal wound to the steamer *Yankee*. Captain Dennis Mugan, his entire crew of 22 and all eight passengers abandoned ship without injury.

In 1988, Bill Campbell dove the *Yankee* and brought up an 18 pound

Diver Gene Howley on the wreck of the *Yankee*. Photo by Brad Sheard.

This 18 pound blackfish was caught
by Bill Campbell in 1988. Photo
by Jack Campbell.

blackfish. Although this is not quite a record fish, it is certainly impressive, especially after hearing the story behind its capture. First of all, Bill didn't even have a spear gun; he was just looking around for lobsters when he found the huge fish amongst some wreckage. Bill took out his dive knife and stabbed the fish, trying to hold it against the sand bottom so it couldn't escape. The fish was so strong that it yanked the knife right out of Bill's hands, and swam away with the knife still in its side. Bill swam after the fish and soon found his knife sitting in the sand. He was amazed that he could actually see a blood trail floating just off the bottom. After imitating a blood hound for a few minutes, he relocated his prized fish wedged between two steel hull plates. A photograph of Bill and his fish appeared in the next issue of the LONG ISLAND FISHERMAN Magazine.

Today, the *Yankee* is in 125 to 135 feet of water 18 miles out of Fire Island Inlet. He twin boilers, single triple expansion engine and steel four bladed propeller all lie in a straight line. Most of her wreckage is flattened out, but she is still an excellent lobstering wreck.

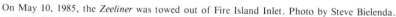

ZEELINER

In 1958, the *Zeeliner* was purchased from the U.S. government for $29,000 and added to the Zee Line ferry fleet. She was 63 feet long and was said to originally be a WW 11 PT boat.

On May 10, 1985, the *Zeeliner* was towed out of Fire Island Inlet. Photo by Steve Bielenda.

Her valves were opened and she slowly filled with sea water. Photo by Steve Bielenda.

The *Zeeliner* was taken out of commission and then contracted by Sea Tow, Inc. to be sunk as an artificial reef. She was then stripped of useful machinery and approved for sinking by the Department of Conservation.

On May 10, 1985, the *Zeeliner* was towed out of Fire Island Inlet where her valves were opened, but four hours later the *Zeeliner* still hadn't sunk. Due to a heavy sea, the smaller Sea Tow, Inc. boats were forced to return to port leaving the *Zeeliner* floating just below the surface, tied to the research vessel, Wahoo. By nightfall and with an even heavier sea, the Wahoo anchored her to the bottom and also returned to port.

It was not until two weeks later that Larry Listing of the vessel, Pegleg, located the sunken ferry. She had drifted a full mile east before finally sinking in 75 feet of water.

The new artificial fish haven was first commercially fished by the vessel, Captain Joseph. Only four months after the *Zeeliner* sunk, fishermen anchored above her reported to have had one of their best fishing days ever.

In 1986, after enduring some powerful winter storms, this wreck has been reduced to an engine and very small debris field. In fact, it was thought that the wreck was completely gone until Larry Listing relocated her with the use of side scan sonar.

This photo was taken two weeks after the *Zeeliner* sunk. Photo by Tim Nargi.

Dan Berg, Rick Schwarz and Dennis Berg aboard the *Wreck Valley*. Photo courtesy Hank Garvin.

SOURCES OF SHIPWRECK INFORMATION

Dossin Museum
Belle Isle
Detroit, Michigan 48207

Library of Congress
Geography and Map Division
Washington, D.C. 20540

Mariners Museum Library
Newport News, Virginia 23606

National Archives and Records Service
8th and Pennsylvania Avenues, MW
Washington, DC 20408

National Maritime Museum
Greenwich
London SE109NF

Naval Historical Center (SH)
Building 220-2
Washington Navy Yard
Washington, D.C. 20374

Peabody Museum of Salem
Phillips Library
East India Square
Salem, Mass 01970

Smithsonian Institution
Museum of American History
Washington, D.C. 20560

Steamship Historical Society of America
University of Baltimore Library
1420 Maryland Avenue
Baltimore, Md 21201

SUGGESTED READING

Berg, Daniel
  Shore Diver
  Aqua Explorers, Inc. (1987)

Berg, Daniel
  Wreck Valley
  Aqua Explorers, Inc. (1986)

Berg, Daniel and Denise
  Tropical Shipwrecks
  Aqua Explorers, Inc. (1989)

Berman, Bruce
  Encyclopedia of American Shipwrecks
  Mariners Press (1972)

Blout, Steve
  The Bahamas Nassau and New Providence Island
  Pisces Books (1985)

Cohen, Shlomo
  Bahamas Diver's Guide
  Seapen Books (1977)

Davis, Bill
  Shipwrecks off the Central New Jersey Coast
  (1987)

Dethlefsen, Edwin
  Whidah
  Seafarers Heritage Library (1984)

Farb, Roderick
  Shipwrecks
  Menasha Ridge Press (1985)

Fish, John Perry
Unfinished Voyages
Lower Cape Publishing (1989)

Fowles, John
Shipwreck
Little, Brown and Co. (1974)

Gentile, Gary
Advanced Wreck Diving Guide
Cornell Maritime Press (1988)

Gentile, Gary
Andrea Doria
Gary Gentile Productions (1989)

Gentile, Gary
U.S.S. San Diego
Gary Gentile Productions (1989)

Gentile, Gary
Shipwrecks Of New Jersey
Sea Sports Publications (1988)

Haws, Duncan
Merchant Fleets in Profile, Vol II
(1979)

Hocking, Charles
Dictionary of Disasters at Sea During the Age of Steam
Lloyd's Register of Shipping (1969)

Keatts, Henry. and Farr, George
Dive into History U-Boats
American Merchant Marine Museum Press (1986)

Keatts, Henry and Farr, George
Dive into History, Warships
Gulf Publishers Co (1990)

Keatts, Henry
New England's Legacy of Shipwrecks
American Merchant Marine Museum Press (1988)

Kludas, Arnold
Great Passenger Ships of the World
Patrick Stephens

Lewbel, George
Bonaire Curacao and Aruba
Pisces Book (1984)

Lonsdale, Adrian L. and Kaplan, H.R.
A Guide to Sunken Ships in American Waters
Compass Publications, (1964)

Mathewson, Duncan
Treasure of the Atocha
Pisces Books (1986)

Marler, George and Luana
The Royal Mail Steamer Rhone
Marler Publications Ltd (1978)

Marx, Robert
Shipwrecks in the Americas
Bonanza Books (1983)

Metery, Michel
Tamaya
(1984)

Morris, Paul and Quinn, William
Shipwrecks in New York Waters
Parnassus Imprints (1989)

Overshiner, Elwyn
Course 095 to Eternity
Elwyn E. Overshiner (1980)

Peterson, Mendal
History Under the Sea
Mendel Peterson (1973)

Quinn, William
Shipwrecks around Cape Cod
Lower Cape Publishing Co. (1973)

Quinn, William
Shipwrecks around New England
Lower Cape Publishing Co. (1979)

Seibold, David and Adams, Charles
Shipwrecks off Ocean City
(1986)

Seibold, David and Adams, Charles
Shipwrecks Sea Stories & Legends of the Delaware Coast
Exeter House Books (1989)

Smith, Eugene
Passenger Ships of the World Past and Present
George H. Dean Company (1978)

Zarzynski, Joseph
Monster Wrecks of Loch Ness and Lake Champlain
M-Z Information. (1986)

Loran "C" List

Acara	26801.4	Black Point	14456.2
	43750.8		43938.5
Ajace	26956.6**	Black Warrior	26951.8
	43754.1		43755.3
Andrea Doria	25147.7	Bronx Queen	26968.8
	43480.7		43735.1
Arundo	26796.9	Brunette	26916.4
	43534.4		43476.0
Asfalto	26831.2	Charlemagne Tower	
	43620.8		26921.8
			43339.2
Ayuruoca	26841.5		
	43547.3	Charles Dunlap	26929.8*
			43755.2
Ba Wreck	26874.7		
	43619.6	Choapa	26863.6
			43590.8
Balaena	26799.8		
	43521.8	Coal Wreck	26796.4
			43671.7
Bald Eagle	26831.4		
	43640.3	Coimbra	26203.6
			43576.6
U.S.S. Bass	14560.8		
	43817.3	Cornelia Soule	26954.7
			43759.1
Bidevind	26357.6		
	43280.5	Delaware	26928.4
			43467.5

Dodger	26617.9 43673.4	Hylton Castle	26569.4 43695.3
Dragger	26795.6 43725.9	Iberia	26855.8 43736.3
Drumelzier	26674.1 43754.3	Immaculata	26801.8 43583.8
Dunlap	N/A	Ioannis P. Goulandris	26853.8 43576.9
Durley Chine	26308.1 43310.6	Irma C	26660.5 43571.8
Edwin Duke	26781.5 43737.1	John C. Fitzpatrick	26135.6 43770.4
Eureka	26772.2 43600.2	Kenosha	26598.9 43644.8
Fran S	26873.6 43733.6	Lana Carol	26859.9 43419.7
Gate City	26420.6 43790.3	Lillian	26697.0 43419.4
G&D	26671.4 43574.3	Linda	26508.8 43601.2
Great Isaac	26840.9 43195.2	Lizzie D	26828.8 43696.5
Gulftrade	26821.3 43318.3	Margaret	26901.2 43756.5
Howard	26773.7 43753.4		

Maurice Tracy	26890.1	Pinta	26880.5
	43356.9		43564.1
Mistletoe	26933.3	Pipe Barge	26869.7
	43747.6		43738.6
Mohawk	26878.1	Princess Anne	26968.3*
	43440.0		43758.1
		Rascal	N/A
R.C. Mohawk	26867.5		
	43670.9	Reggie	26593.9
			43658.9
Ocean Prince	26631.1	Relief Ship	26903.5
	43733.5		43695.6
Oregon	26453.1	Republic	14073.0
	43676.5		43453.6
Panther	26248.7	R.P. Resor	26638.3
	43802.0		43277.1
Patrice McAllister	26930.4	Rickseckers	26913.0
	43061.5		43727.1
Pauline Marie	26895.4	Robert A. Snow	26964.3
	42944.0		43759.8
Pentland Firth	26922.5	Roda	26741.5
	43682.0		43756.4
Persephone	26897.1	USS San Diego	26543.3
	43287.1		43692.9
Peter Rickmers	26786.5	Sandy Hook	26908.2
	43754.1**		43700.5

Sommerstad	26425.2 43456.5	U-853	25776.1 43824.8
Spartan	26910.8 43491.1	Varanger	26825.5 42803.7
Steamship	26932.4 43707.0	Wolcott	26518.7 43713.0
Steel Wreck	26794.3 43687.1	Yankee	26609.5 43592.0
Stolt Dagali	26787.6 43484.3	Zeeliner	26622.9 43735.8
Stone Barge	26782.1 43728.3		
Suffolk	25644.7 43726.0		
USS Tarantula	26608.9 43609.6		
Texas Tower	26313.0 43267.8		
Three Sisters	26791.6 43642.1		
Tolten	26815.9 43360.1		
USS Turner	26936.4 43725.5		

* The shipwreck located on this sight has never been positively identified.

** This wreck no longer protrudes from the sea bottom. An approximate Loran location was interpolated from known facts.

INDEX

Other Products Available From Aqua Explorers Inc.

TROPICAL SHIPWRECKS

This exciting book by Daniel and Denise Berg was designed for the travelling diver who's interested in shipwrecks. *Tropical Shipwrecks* contains a wealth of information such as; aquatic life, currents, bottom composition, depth, visibility, and the history and present condition of 135 shipwrecks spread over 35 islands in the Bahamas and Caribbean. The text is heavily illustrated in full color, many of the photographs have never before been published. Copies available for $16.95

WRECK VALLEY

The original version of Daniel Berg's *Wreck Valley* book is available only while supplies last. The history and legend of 58 shipwrecks all located off Long Island N.Y.'s South Shore are explored in this 84 page softcover book. The original *Wreck Valley* book has 51 modern and historic photographs, 14 drawings and six maps. Copies available for $12.95

LORAN "C" LIST

Wreck Valleys shipwreck locations finally disclosed. Our *Loran "C" List*, by Daniel Berg and Steve Bielenda, was designed to be a weather proof tool for fishermen and divers alike. On this list you will find not only over 60 accurate loran numbers, but also wrecks depth and reference page number where historical information can be found in the orginal *Wreck Valley* book. Available for $14.95

SHORE DIVER

Over 40 Long Island N.Y. beach dive locations are described and explored in detail in this book titled *Shore Diver*, by Daniel Berg.

This illustrated 96 page softcover book contains a topside photograph of each location, two historic ship photographs, 15 under water photographs, eight maps plus pertinent information such as easy to follow street directions, depth of water, bottom composition, currents and overall dive conditions. Copies available for $12.95

GRAND CAYMAN SHIPWRECK VIDEO

Aqua Explorers, Inc., recently completed a documentary, filmed by veteran wreck divers author Daniel Berg and Steve Bielenda, on the shipwrecks of Grand Cayman. This one hour video serves as a vacationing sport diver's guide to diving Cayman's shipwrecks. Historical information on each wreck is included as well as topside shots and underwater footage of the Gamma, Callie, Balboa, Oro Verde, Carrie Lee, and Kirk Pride.

Also captured on video: a diver petting a 300 pound grouper; catching a eight pound rock lobster; and penetrating deep inside the Ore Verde. A two-man submersible allowed film makers to record the 800 foot deep wreck of the Kirk Pride. Available for $39.95

NORTH ATLANTIC SHIPWRECK ART

Many of the underwater sketches contained in this text, including the Andrea Doria, Great Isaac, Stolt Dagali and Texas Tower are available on heavy grade parchment. Hang these fine renderings in your home, apartment or office and show your family and friends where you disappear to on the weekends. For a complete flyer on sketches send A.S.A.S.E. To: *Shipwreck Drawings, 1111 Glenview St, Phila, PA, 19111*

WRECK SKETCHES

Wreck Valley shipwreck sketches drawn by Daniel Berg are available direct from Aqua Explorers. The following are reproduced on 8 × 10 parchment paper. Bronx Queen, Cornelia Soule, Dragger, Edwin Duke, Fran S, Iberia, Kenosha, Lizzie D, Mistletoe, R.C Mohawk, Pipe Barge, Relief Ship, and Sandy Hook. Available for $10.00 ea. or any six for $30.00

DIVE INTO HISTORY, U-BOATS

This book, by Hank Keatts and George Farr, traces the development of the U-Boat from its inception. This 183 page, hardcover text is heavily illustrated with 200 photographs many in full color and has specific emphasis on U-Boats sunk in US waters within the range of Scuba. Retail $29.95

NEW ENGLAND'S LEGACY OF SHIPWRECKS

This 164 page softcover book, by Hank Keatts, covers the history and present condition of 30 shipwrecks from Block Island to Portland, Maine. *Legacy Of Shipwrecks* is heavily illustrated with over 160 photographs, 104 are in full color. Retail $16.95

ADVANCED WRECK DIVING GUIDE

This 136 page softcover book, by Gary Gentile, covers the approach, safety techniques, penetration, decompression as well as artifact recovery and restoration. Retail $12.95

SHIPWRECKS OF NEW JERSEY

This 172 page softcover text, by Gary Gentile, covers the history of 80 New Jersey shipwrecks. This book also contains exact Loran locations. Retail $14.95

ANDREA DORIA DIVE TO AN ERA

Dive To An Era, by Gary Gentile, is a heavily illustrated, 160 page hardcover book that covers not only the history but the present condition of this magnificent shipwreck. Over 160 color photographs. Retail $25.00

WONDERS OF THE DEEP

Wonders Of The Deep, Underwater Bermuda is a 9×12, 115 page hardcover book with over 112 beautiful underwater photographs. Explore the wonders of Bermuda's shipwrecks and reefs in this fascinating text. Retail $39.95

SHIPWRECKS OF SOUTHERN CALIFORNIA

The history and present condition of 50 wrecks sunk from Surf to San Diego are covered in this 202 page, softcover book by Bonnie Cardone and Patrick Smith. Retail $12.95

SHIPWRECKS

Diving the Graveyard of the Altantic by Roderick Farb. A 265 page, comprehensive guide to North Carolina shipwrecks, their history, photographs of their remains, and how to dive them. This softcover book is a must for anyone who plans on diving the area. Retail $12.95

UNDERWATER PARADISE

The Worlds Best Diving Sites. Travel to seven of the worlds greatest diving sites, places as far as the Red Sea and Papaua, New Guinea. This text is 192 pages, 8 × 11, and has 150 color photographs. Retail $39.95

ORDERING INFORMATION

* Send **Check** or **Money Order.**
* Please include, name, address, and phone #
* **N.Y. residents add 8% sales tax.**
* Postage, Include $2.00 for first book and 50 cents for each additional book.

Aqua Explorers, Inc. distributes a full line of over 35 different book titles, to divers and dive stores. Please send for our complete flyer of dive books. Remember we specialize in Shipwreck publications.

Aqua Explorers Inc.
P.O. Box 116
East Rockaway N.Y. 11518
Phone (516) 868–2658